Joni

WOMEN OF FAITH SERIES

Amy Carmichael
Corrie ten Boom
Florence Nightingale
Gladys Aylward
Hannah Whitall Smith
Isobel Kuhn
Mary Slessor
Joni

MEN OF FAITH SERIES

Borden of Yale
Brother Andrew
C. S. Lewis
Charles Finney
Charles Spurgeon
Eric Liddell
George Muller
Hudson Taylor
Jim Elliot
Jonathan Goforth
John Hyde
John Wesley
Martin Luther
Samuel Morris
Terry Waite
William Carey
William Booth

John and Betty Stam

Joni

Kathleen White

BETHANY HOUSE PUBLISHERS
MINNEAPOLIS, MINNESOTA 55438

Joni
Kathleen White

Library of Congress Catalog Card Number 93–74541

ISBN 1–55661–364–4

The author asserts the moral right to be identified as the
author of his work.
Originally published in English by Marshall, Morgan & Scott
Publications Ltd. (now part of HarperCollins Publishers, Ltd.)
under the title *Joni*,
© 1993 (Kathleen White).

Cover by Dan Thornberg,
Bethany House Publishers staff artist.

Published by Bethany House Publishers
A Ministry of Bethany Fellowship, Inc.
11300 Hampshire Ave. South
Minneapolis, MN 55438

Printed in the United States of America

1

*T*he usual midweek silence of the Church of All Souls, Langham Place in London was interrupted by visitors trying hard to contain their excitement. It was a summer's day in 1987 and the auditorium was filled. Suppressed whispers filled the room while newcomers hurried to find one of the few remaining seats. Women wearing brightly colored clothing exchanged knowing smiles with friends across the aisles. Men, being in the minority but no less enthused about the program that was about to start, sat quietly in their contrasting dark suits.

The shops on nearby Oxford Street or the art galleries and museums would have been the usual attraction for such a crowd. But a very special guest to the church changed the day's routine. She was special enough to bring some people to the church simply out of curiosity. Some came because they had already read her gripping life story and wanted to see her now in person. Still others came for the privilege of enjoying her dynamic testimony and message a second time.

The atmosphere of the auditorium changed abruptly as they heard the whine of a small motor off stage. The hubbub died down. Stragglers hurried to find a seat. One could sense the audience's curiosity. *What would this woman look like who had experienced so much since her paralyzing accident twenty years ago? What would her active pace of life have done to her spirit, her demeanor? Would she look resigned, careworn, her face etched with lines of suffering?*

As she reached the center of the platform, an almost audible gasp of surprise went up from the audience. Joni Eareckson Tada's face glowed with vitality. Her smile and pretty features disarmed the expectations of everyone except for those who had seen her before. She was dressed simply, yet fashionably, in clothes that enhanced her personality rather than draw attention to her disability. Her full, fair hair shone under the lights of the stage. Her physical beauty was stunning, captivating everyone.

But it was not Joni's mission that day, nor had it been her life's mission, to draw attention to herself. Through her testimony and through her song, Joni made it clear that attention was to be drawn to her Lord. She spoke with sincerity and conviction on the theme from Romans 8:28: "All things work together for good to those that love God and are called according to His purpose."

Later in the program, Joni was joined on stage by her husband, Ken. Ken's dark hair and tall, muscular body was a striking contrast to Joni's. They teased and spoke with each other lovingly. The audience was left with the impression that the relationship must have been a healthy one, despite the difficulties that would naturally come with Joni's disability. One could not tell from looking at them that four out of five marriages similar to Ken and Joni's end in divorce. By the end of the afternoon, it was clear in everyone's mind why Joni had come. Comments such as, "She's not on an ego trip," "She's not promoting herself," "She's sincere and cares about people," were heard often as people left the auditorium and lined up at the book stalls. Joni had come to praise God and to inspire others.

Born in Baltimore, Maryland in 1950 as the youngest

of four sisters, Joni enjoyed her growing years in a spacious and comfortable home. Life took a traumatic turn when she became paralyzed as a result of a diving accident. A casual dive from a raft crushed the vertebrae in her neck and any dreams she had for the future. That "accident" and the subsequent events of her life would underscore for everyone the fact that God does indeed have a plan for His people—a plan that is very different for each person.

God's unique plan for Joni had its beginnings long before the diving accident. To understand Joni's life one needs to know the story of her parents, Johnny and Lindy. Their story is also a fascinating example of how God uses circumstances and people in unique ways.

Johnny Eareckson was not a wealthy man nor was he born with a silver spoon in his mouth. He worked hard all of his life, at times under severe conditions. His father, who owned a coal mining business, never pampered Johnny. As soon as he was old enough, he was made to groom and feed the heavy cart-horses that pulled the coal wagons through the busy streets of town.

Johnny worked for his father in the early morning and in the evening. Between working hours, he went to school and completed his homework without grumbling. Johnny relished the challenge of work and study in contrast to many boys his age. He enjoyed his studies as much as he enjoyed working with horses. The simple enjoyment of work made every experience—academic or vocational—a positive and successful one.

In addition to work and study, Johnny tackled all opportunities with enthusiasm. His talents and leisure interests were so diverse—from sculpture and painting to building and sailing. He was also successful as an Olympic wrestler.

Johnny's love for such a variety of activities had not

been developed quickly nor under easy conditions. When the Great Depression hit America hard in the 1920s, he earned a living by carving wood that had been thrown away at construction sites. Though he was a thinker, he knew that one needed to work with one's hands and to do whatever it took to make one's way in life under difficult circumstances. An incident Joni recalls from her memory exemplifies such an attitude.

A lovely barn on their property, built by Pennsylvania Dutch builders and used as his workshop, was deliberately set on fire by an arsonist. Working day and night he reconstructed the barn, salvaging very little from the ashes.

Incredibly, the rebuilt barn was burned down again two years later. Undaunted by the second disaster, Johnny rebuilt it again from the foundation stones up.

Lindy Landwehr was a member of the church youth group that Johnny sponsored. "Cap'n John," as he was called, led the groups on many camping trips, including one to the famous Mt. Rushmore, which has the likenesses of four U.S. presidents carved in its side. Lindy, in fact, was given the opportunity of carving out a portion of George Washington's nose with a jack hammer on the trip!

Johnny fell in love with Lindy, fifteen years his junior, and the two were married in 1940. Johnny constructed a home made from timbers of an old sailing ship and boulders from a wall that was being demolished near their homesite.

Lindy served as an equally important guide in Joni's life. Skilled in athletics such as swimming and tennis, she passed on her love of competition and zest for life to all of her daughters. Even in her 70s, Lindy still plays tennis and often travels with Joni on whirlwind tours.

Despite the intensity with which Johnny and Lindy approached life, neither parent was interested solely in what their four daughters could achieve. The girls were nurtured in a warm and loving family environment. Affection and supportive words helped each one grow in self-confidence. Family relationships were precious, and close friendships were valued highly.

Family activities such as hiking and horseback riding served as opportunities to strengthen the bonds of the family in addition to teaching the girls needed character traits.

Writing in one of her books, Joni shared some happy childhood memories with her readers. "As you know, when I was on my feet, I loved riding, especially when I was little. When I was finally big enough to ride my own pony, I just had to keep up with my older sisters on their big horses . . . I had to gallop twice as fast to keep up with everybody else."

"Do you remember, Joni?" her dad had once asked. "You were only four years old, but the whole family rode a hundred miles on horseback from Laramie to Cheyenne."

Those rides with Dad were also fun because he pointed out animal tracks, taught the girls to listen for bird calls, pointed out changing rock formations, and different plants and trees. Joni's love for God's nature was deeply rooted as a result.

Joni's love for her sisters was also nurtured through such experiences. She has often shared memories of her love for them in several of her books. "There was nobody who could match the importance of my three older sisters . . . sure, we had our share of scuffles . . . but I was always glad to be together with them. I loved posing for photographs with them. I glowed with pleasure when they'd say something nice about me. There's something wonderful about sharing the same genetics with another person—the same parents, roots, background, memories, history—and in a sense, flesh and blood."

All the Eareckson sisters retained this interest in their roots. Years later when they were all married, they took a trip to trace one branch of their family tree. Following an old map passed on to them, they tracked down the original Eareckson homestead, deserted and desolate. They found two moss-covered stones carved with the names of Benjamin and Elizabeth on the property. The thrill of tracing one's roots and finding such evidence strengthened their bond with their heritage.

Bonding between sisters took various forms, including the raising of calves. Feeding and cleaning were always messy chores, but the girls took great pleasure and pride in their responsibilities. Joni and Kathy also enjoyed building a tree house, far from prying eyes.

Trips to Uncle Doug and Auntie Fran on their farm fifty miles away made for special family times. The fun would begin with milking the cows and continue through the morning with a mock battle in the fields where they used overripe tomatoes as ammunition. Mom could have done without that kind of bonding, as the girls would return to lunch covered in bright red stains!

Christmas celebrations on the farm were always special. "Christmas began the day after Thanksgiving in November and ran nonstop to December 25. There were parties and plays, dances and dates, decorating, baking, and shopping."

Joni's school was also set in a country environment. Streams and many beautiful trees surrounded the campus. Joni took advantage of the athletic program as well, becoming captain of her lacrosse team in high school.

Joni's life was filled with so many opportunities and love that one would wonder if any teenager would find need for anything more. She was an attractive girl, an athletic member of the school community, popular with friends, and supported by an affectionate family. And yet something was missing—something that prompted her to beg her mother to allow her to attend a Christian outreach ministry called Young Life.

The first meeting was not what Joni had expected. While she sought some answers to minor problems experienced by every teenager, the leader of the group had quite another set of answers in mind. Carl Nelson told the kids that night, "Sin is wrong and hateful to God. But not one of us, however hard we may try, can live according to God's standards. We desperately need help outside ourselves!"

Carl's message shook Joni. Her life had been filled with activity. It had also been filled with trying harder—determination, commitment, and independence as key values. Her parents were regular church members, and she had been taught about the love of God from early childhood. But it hadn't made a great impact on her. Now someone was telling her she could not do anything to deal with her problem of sin.

Joni was disturbed by Carl's message but she did not reject it. A sinner? "Wow, I'd never thought of it like that before!" She decided she would not try to deceive herself or anyone else. "That's true, I can't save myself, and God cared enough to send His only Son to die on my behalf." She turned to God with a simple prayer asking for forgiveness and promised to live her life God's way from that time on.

Joni was obedient to her commitment and entered into her relationship with Christ as enthusiastically as she had other activities. Her friends knew of her decision in simple, declarative exclamations—"I've asked Jesus to take over my life!" And challenges to share her faith with others were accepted promptly.

Joni's response to God's claim on her life was enthusiastic but did not maintain the same intensity in the months that followed. Reflecting on the experience years later, Joni saw that Christian activities such as singing in the choir or summer camp began to replace her relationship with God. She had not come to know God any more personally than she had when she first gave her life to Him. He was slowly being squeezed out of her life by worthwhile activities.

As her relationship with God lessened, her relationship with a boy named Jason grew. Tall, handsome, and full of fun, Joni fell for him easily. They dated often. Bible study and prayer time also became a regular part of their life and the topic of marriage at some time in the future came up frequently.

Joni's relationship with Jason grew prematurely. The more time they spent alone, the more difficult they found it to hold back from expressing their love for each other physically. In desperation, Joni brought the matter out into the open.

"Jason, we've just got to stop seeing each other. It's too much of a strain, and we're going to sin if we go on like this. Please understand. I'm finding it hard enough to ask you."

Jason responded as a gentlemen, although the decision hurt them both. "Tell you what, Joni. How about going around with my friend Dick for a while? He's a good friend of mine and I know he'll look after you well. It'll give us a bit of breathing space."

Joni agreed and her life seemed a little easier. Dick was a steady Christian boy who was good company and who made few emotional demands on her. She had been accepted at Western Maryland College for the fall and she hoped that the change would help even further.

It appeared so on the surface, but Joni began to feel

undercurrents of disquiet as she completed her last semester of high school. She slackened her studies and her grades dropped. Her parents' observations about her change annoyed her even more and she began to resent them. She had solved the problem with Jason but realized she was becoming too possessive with Dick.

It's no good, Joni, she told herself firmly one day. *In two years you've gone nowhere as a Christian. There's just got to be a better way.*

Turning to God, she begged Him fervently one night as she lay in bed. "It's up to you now, God. I'm making no headway. Do anything to my life, turn it right around if you like. But I want to start living your way."

God's prompting on Joni's heart was only the beginning of His plan.

2

God used a hot day in July of 1967 to answer Joni's prayer. No one could foresee the events that would unfold that day nor in the years to come. The day and setting was ordinary—sweltering heat, teenagers at the beach, Chesapeake Bay, a raft, and a rock too close to the surface to be considered safe.

Joni, her sister Kathy, and Kathy's boyfriend, Butch, drove to the bay to enjoy the cool water and a picnic together. The day was filled with typical activities, and it was not until late in the day that the three began to have thoughts of going home. There would be just one more swim before packing the gear and heading home for supper. Joni stood at the edge of the raft that was anchored some distance offshore. The surface of the water reflected all light, hiding whatever might be under the surface. She arched her back forward as she sprang up in an athletic dive. The cold water was invigorating as she broke the surface with her arms.

The cool sensation was shattered quickly as her head struck a rock. Her body went out of control and she found herself on the bottom, her arms tightly pinned across her chest.

There was no motion, no panic, and no pain. There was

nothing but the current of the bay as it shifted her back and forth.

Joni never lost consciousness. Her mind raced to determine what could have happened and planned desperately some means of escape. *How long could I stay under water like this? What is my problem? How come I can't move? And most important, has anyone noticed l haven't come back to the surface?*

There were no answers to most of her questions. Only one of them caused her to panic. No one would be on the lookout for danger when it came to Joni! She was an experienced swimmer and diver, and there would be no reason to keep track of her whereabouts.

The panic deepened. *Dear God! I don't want to die yet.* She tried desperately to kick her legs but there was no response. Her lungs were almost bursting and she knew she couldn't hold out much longer. Random memories of her family flashed through her mind.

That's what people say it's like when you're near to drowning, thought Joni in despair. *Won't anyone come to rescue me?*

The answer came within seconds as she began to hear her name being called over and over again. A dark shadow was swimming above her that she couldn't identify but assumed to be Kathy's. Would she make it in time?

Kathy grabbed hold of Joni but struggled to bring her to the surface. Joni's dead weight gave no assistance. Joni blacked out for a split second until her face broke the surface of the water where she was able to gulp fresh air.

She weakly stammered the words, "Thank you, God."

Kathy supported her in the water as she led Joni on her back toward the beach.

"You okay, Joni?" she asked anxiously. Joni's limbs hung helpless, unable to help in her own rescue.

Kathy realized she had a crisis on her hands, so she quickly commandeered an inflatable raft from another swimmer. Once in shallow water, she dragged Joni onto the beach.

The beach seemed a logical place to stand, and so Joni made an attempt. There was still no movement in Joni's legs or arms. Curious and helpful bystanders gathered around. They were too much for Joni.

"Kathy, get them to go, please."

She knew they only meant well, but their stares and comments embarrassed her. She wanted to be left alone.

"I can't move, Kathy!" Panic began to settle in Joni's voice as Kathy made attempts to squeeze Joni's arms and legs. There was no sensation. Only when Kathy squeezed Joni's shoulders was there a positive response.

"I can feel that . . . I'm sure I'm going to be all right!"

It was several minutes before rescue workers arrived and loaded Joni onto a stretcher and into an ambulance. Kathy joined Joni in the ambulance and Butch followed in his car.

Joni was eager to apologize to the nurse who sat next to her in the ambulance. "I'm sorry to cause so much fuss. I'll be fine shortly when the numbness wears off."

The eerie noise of the siren's alarm made it impossible to pray coherently. And Joni was confused and disoriented. A few phrases from the twenty-third Psalm floated through her mind, heartwarming and comforting in the bizarre situation in which she found herself. Though unsure of the words, she was sure that God would let no lasting harm come to her.

The sun had set by the time they arrived at the hospital. Though her body could not feel anything, she nevertheless sensed a chill as they moved from the ambulance into the emergency room. She was placed on the examining table surrounded by curtains on three sides.

Joni asked urgent questions of the nurse but received no reply—either of reassurance or comfort. Another nurse wrote down details of her name, address, and telephone on a clipboard.

Yet another nurse stepped forward with a large pair of scissors in her hand and proceeded to cut off Joni's bathing suit.

"Hey! You can't do that!" Joni protested in vain. The nurse continued her task until the swimsuit was cut in several pieces and then thrown into the wastebin. It was the first of many indignities she would experience in the days that followed on her journey through the world of medicine.

The emergency room doctor arrived and began testing Joni's responses with sharp jabs on her skin. Only her shoulders reacted to the probing. Feet, legs, arms, and wrists remained numb and immobile.

After consulting with other medical staff, the doctor injected anesthetic for the next procedure—the drilling of her skull for traction. Still in disbelief over the severity of her situation, Joni angrily cried out as the doctor began shaving her head with electric clippers.

"No! Please, not my hair!"

The procedure continued without regard for Joni's cries. Clumps of hair, still wet from swimming, fell to the floor.

After shampooing the scalp, the doctor began drilling into her skull. The anesthetic had taken effect for the pain but Joni was still conscious at this point, very aware of each step and frightened at the implications. It was several more minutes before the drowsiness from the anesthetic took over and forced her to sleep. She would drift in and out of the drug-induced sleep for the next several days, giving her body and the doctors the opportunity to work un-impeded by Joni's fears.

Her family had no such respite. Each moment was spent wondering anxiously about Joni's condition and future. They were grateful she had been saved from death. But the nightmare she now entered was equally trying for the family. They longed for answers from doctors but none were forthcoming. As each day passed, hopes for a miracle disappeared. They struggled with the reality that Joni might never again be the lively, energetic extrovert they had come to love. Johnny visited as often as he could during the first few days. Lindy stayed by her daughter's side for four straight days without going home, napping in the chair in fitful intervals. Frequent bulletins went out to Joni's sisters. Kathy was a frequent visitor to the ward during the early days. Linda, the oldest with three children of her own, visited as often as she could along with Jay who also had a child. Jay's visits were difficult for her, as she needed to hide the news of her failing marriage from the rest of the family. The family's current crisis was Joni. Jay's would have to wait. The anxieties and questions that had been the sole property of the family soon became Joni's as she regained full consciousness. The implications of her situation were difficult to bear for the lively seventeen-year-old. Years later Joni commented about those days, "It's tough being a teenager. It's even tougher when you're seventeen and face life in a wheelchair . . . 'Life on my feet' stopped when I was seventeen."

Her questions were not always philosophical in those first weeks of being disabled. "Where am I? And why am I hanging upside down from my bed over the floor?"

"You're in ICU—Intensive Care Unit—and you're on a Stryker Frame," Joni was told. The Stryker Frame was a bed held at two ends by pivots. Joni would be strapped in the bed and every two hours a nurse would flip the bed over, leaving Joni either suspended over the floor or facing a dull, flat ceiling. Neither view provided the distractions she would need during the endless hours of waiting.

Joni was not alone in her boredom. Six other patients in ICU—all from serious accidents—helped Joni realize that her situation was not exclusive. Though unable to see each other, the patients were able to provide one another some moral support.

Joni connected with one patient in particular. Tom was more severely disabled and required a respirator in order to breathe. The two struck up a "conversation" by using the nurses as couriers. The nurses encouraged the relationship as a way of bolstering Joni's and Tom's spirits and were more than happy to write notes for them. Tom had also been in a diving accident, which served as an instant point of reference for Joni.

Tom's respirator stopped suddenly one evening. Joni lay in a sweat of terror and frustration because she could not run to the rescue. Alert staff rushed to the scene and ordered a new respirator to be delivered. While they waited for the replacement machine, the staff worked frantically to save Tom.

Despite their efforts to provide the needed oxygen, Tom did not make it. The arrival of the new respirator came too late and Joni lost a friend. She lay in her bed, alone, choking with emotion. She hadn't even known what he looked like. He was gone.

3

Tom's death lingered in Joni's thoughts often during the following weeks. The thoughts became self-centered. *What if my treatment failed and I was the next to go? I'm not dependent on a machine, but what if other things went wrong?*

Strapped to the Stryker Frame, there was no place to escape from her questions and fears. Reassurances from the staff meant little. No one told her about her test results or communicated her prognosis. It seemed to her that no progress was being made. And Tom's death was not an isolated event.

Within days of Tom's passing a new patient was brought with similar conditions as Tom's. Joni could see his oxygen tent and bed frame. Terror would seize the young man every time the orderlies came to flip him over.

"You'll be okay," they reassured him. "Just you see."

What the young man saw was anything but okay. He died also, strapped to a metal frame and breathing machine.

Watching a second death so close by led Joni to entertain morbid thoughts. *I know why I'm here now. ICU is the place where people die. You only get to this ward if there's no hope for you. What's to stop me from being next?* Her thoughts were not without merit.

One day while being flipped on the frame, she lost con-

20

sciousness and stopped breathing. The staff successfully revived her, but it was clear to Joni that death was much closer than even across the room in someone else's bed.

From Joni's perspective, it was only a matter of time before she too would die. Like an ostrich, she buried her head in the sand. She was convinced her fate was sealed, and so she shut her ears to what the doctors began to tell her. "They are afraid to tell me things," she concluded. "They won't tell me I'm going to die but I know I am."

Joni's attention turned away from the doctors toward God, albeit with equal doubt and denial. "Why, God? Why are you doing this?" The hospital ward, and God's ears, seemed disinterested in such questions. No one seemed to have any answers.

———

Days passed in the ward with little change except for the patients who came in and out. Some died. Some left for rehabilitation. The only thing constant in the ward was the equipment, staff, and Joni.

By this time it was not only members of her family who visited her. Friends who had only heard secondhand and thirdhand reports were finally allowed in. Many could not hide their sense of shock when they first entered the room and saw Joni.

Joni's boyfriend, Dick, was one of her faithful visitors after the hospital allowed more than just the immediate family into the ward. He hadn't abandoned her in her distress and he always brought a message of hope each time he came. His message was not always accepted.

"Everything works together for good, Joni. It says so in the Bible," he tried to convince her one day.

"You just tell me one good thing about my condition, Dick! I've been here over a month already and I'm still no nearer being let out. I've made no progress at all."

Dick had to admit silently that things did not look good. It was hard seeing Joni unable to move or care for herself. But it did not deter him from making the effort to cheer her up. His efforts included the stretching of hospital rules to unusual lengths.

On one such visit to Joni, Dick snuck up nine flights of the hospital's back stairs. Concealing a bulge in his jacket, he furtively walked past the nurses and into Joni's ward. Once at her bedside, Dick revealed his secret—a gorgeous puppy that eagerly licked Joni's face and wagged its tail. It was just the kind of therapy Joni needed, and though the nurses knew what Dick had done, they did not interrupt the covert activity.

Joni's sister, Jay, also added unusual approaches to the normal hospital visit. If Joni was lying with her face toward the floor, Jay would sprawl out teenage magazines so that Joni could read them and chat with her about them. Jay also brought posters for the ceiling and potted plants to make the room more homelike.

Jason, Joni's previous boyfriend, also visited, though not as frequently as Dick. She could tell that he still cared for her from the tears that welled up in his eyes. Their relationship had cooled since Dick's arrival on the dating scene, but it gave her a bittersweet feeling to realize Jason still had affection for her. His affection, however, carried with it some anger that did nothing to help Joni.

"You've gotta fight like mad, Joni, to get over this. How could a God of love let this happen to you?"

Memories also served as Joni's company during her time in the ward. She relived outings with the family and other activities she thought she could no longer enjoy.

One such activity involved her beloved horse, Tumble-weed. *Would my sisters remember to exercise and groom her while I'm in the hospital? And is Tumbleweed missing me? Does she think I've deserted her?* Joni and Tumbleweed had made a formidable team, winning rosettes at local gymkhanas.

Remembrances of Tumbleweed brought to mind her days with horses as a young child, when she was too small to ride her own horse.

"When we went riding, I sat behind my father on his big horse. With my tiny hands, I'd hang on to his belt for dear life . . . I'd bounce up and down on the back of his saddle, sliding this way and that, but as long as I had a strong hold on that belt, I knew I was safe."

Memories such as this served her well in years to come as she would illustrate in her writings and messages how God looked after His children. With an earthly father like Johnny Eareckson, it was easier to visualize and communicate what her heavenly Father was like. She could appreciate the provision He had made for all His children.

In time, Joni's stay in the ward turned to encouraging thoughts and the future. She paid close attention to what was happening to her and to doing her best. She made as many efforts as possible to ensure that her visits with family involved her facing up toward the ceiling rather than to the floor.

She became aware of her medical situation sometimes through insight, at other times through direct questioning. She observed for example that there were patients in much worse condition than she, and that gave some hope. She also realized her recovery was aided by the stream of visitors and family that rallied around her. It also seemed that a couple of the nurses went out of their way to be extra kind to her.

Direct questions also served to draw Joni more deeply into the process of her rehabilitation.

"I must know exactly what's wrong with me, Dr. Harris," she said one day as he made his rounds. The doctor began to hedge but Joni would not let him.

"Okay, then, Joni, I'll get Dr. Sherill to explain it himself."

It would be several days before Dr. Sherill would be able to meet with Joni. She received further treatments—a bone scan and a myelogram—which knocked her out for a lengthy period of time. When she felt strong enough after the sedation, she finally confronted him.

Dr. Sherill confirmed what she already knew regarding the fact that she had broken her neck. It was the prognosis that interested her the most.

"You're strong, Joni, and unlike many others, you've survived the first four weeks. They're the toughest time."

"So, what's next, Doctor?"

"I'm going to try an operation on your spinal cord to fuse the bones together."

"Wow! That's great. Can you do it as soon as possible?"

As soon as I've had the surgery, Joni promised herself, *I'll be using my arms and legs again.* Joni's parents joined to a lesser degree in Joni's optimism. When the operation was pronounced a success and Joni was moved to a regular ward, they began making plans for her long-term future. They approached Dr. Sherill about college. His answer dashed their hopes completely.

"Joni might possibly use her hands again but her spinal injury is permanent. She'll never walk again."

Joni tried to keep her spirits up as long as her parents remained by her bedside. But she gave way to tears when she was left on her own. *Wouldn't it have been better if I'd died like Tom and the other fellow on the ward? At least it would have spared my parents the shock of hearing that I was permanently disabled.* The future looked too bleak to contemplate with any optimism at that point.

But Joni, determined and energetic as she was, had to find a way to encourage herself. She told herself that she'd walk out of the hospital one day. After all, the doctors could be wrong.

Optimism and despair walked closely together during those days. She walked on an emotional see-saw. Her moods swung from deep depression to moments of elation, when she was convinced everything would sort itself out successfully one day. She tried hard to be positive, but setbacks cropped up just when she felt her feelings were under control.

Mood swings took her in both directions rapidly at times. "God will help me," she told a nurse one day who had come into the room to wipe Joni's tears. Joni had just a half hour earlier pleaded with God to let her die.

Her ups and downs with God's purpose in her accident led her to wrestle with the problem of prayer. She had asked God specifically to give her a new direction in life just before her diving accident. But she didn't like the result. "Is this your idea of an answer? . . . I'll never trust you with another answer again!" she raged.

Years later, Joni confessed in her book *Seeking God*, ". . . many Christians, myself included . . . thoughtlessly meander up to God as though He were a doting old grandfather in the sky, giving out grace as He would pass out chocolate chip cookies." She thought back to all the casual and selfish prayers she used to make for the most trivial of things—a date, her homework, even her personal appearance. She had expected instant answers to instant prayers, and so she could not handle God's response to her heart-felt plea regarding her entire future.

Joni's rehabilitation began upon her transfer to the new ward. Physically, she had a great deal of ground to make up. And to build up her strength, she needed to stock up on good, nourishing food. She had been fed intravenously or fed liquids for a month and her weight had plummeted. The hospital chef bent over backwards to tempt Joni with her favorite foods, but she could hardly swallow a crumb. Side effects from the drugs involved in her treatment made her feel sick and gave her nightmares.

Treatments and surgery during the previous month took a toll on her appearance. First-time visitors were often unable to bear what they saw of Joni. Though Joni was always glad to see them and attempted to make them feel as comfortable as possible, they had no idea what to expect and their reactions were sometimes rude.

On one occasion two visitors came together, entered the room, and then promptly rushed out of the room.

What do I really look like? Joni asked herself. It was her friend Jackie who provided the answer.

"Fetch my mirror, please," Joni asked Jackie one day after the two visitors had run out of the room at the sight of her.

Jackie hedged nervously, trying to put her off. Joni persisted . . . and then wished she hadn't. She was totally unprepared for the reflection that met her eyes. It was far, far worse than she had imagined.

Her scalp was still bald from the first operation. Her teeth were discolored from the huge amount of drugs she was forced to take. Her lusterless eyes were sunk deep in her cadaverous face. There was little resemblance to the former Joni who had been an alert, vigorous girl glowing with health and energy. Her eyes used to sparkle and her hair used to shine in the sunlight as she raced across the ranch on her horse, Tumbleweed.

"Why have you done this to me, Lord?" she cried in anguish. Her spirits hit an all-time low at that moment. What was there to live for now?

4

J ackie had no answer for Joni. She sobbed as she held the mirror to Joni's face and felt the shock and anger that Joni felt.

Joni answered her own question in desperation.

"Jackie, you've got to do something. I'm dying anyway. Give me an overdose. Put me out of my misery."

Jackie scolded her, shocked beyond belief that Joni would entertain such thoughts or even ask her for her help. But she was torn in two directions. *What was the right thing to do?* Theirs was not a superficial friendship. If anything, Jackie cared too much and suffered with Joni when she saw what Joni had to undergo day after day, week after week. Jackie, too, wondered if there was any hope. Now that a month or more had past and Joni's appearance looked so bleak, was there any hope for improvement?

Joni broke into Jackie's thoughts.

"Slash my wrists, then. There's no feeling there, so I wouldn't have any pain. Please, please, Jackie."

"I can't, Joni. I'm sorry but I just can't. Don't ask me again."

Despite Jackie's protests, Joni made the same request on several other occasions. She stopped only when she saw how it was upsetting Jackie, but she still felt the desire to die. She hoped that perhaps the hospital staff would

28

make a mistake and do the job that Jackie could not. But no mistakes were forthcoming and that left her feeling angry with herself and frustrated. *If only I had the strength to do it myself!* she fretted.

Jackie did more than refuse Joni's requests. She set about with greater energy to bring hope to Joni. She worked hard to improve Joni's appearance through grooming. She also brought new interests into Joni's life.

Jackie's ministry was not lost on Joni. After sharply attacking Jackie for dropping something on the floor, Joni was caught up short and confessed her bad attitude.

"Jackie, I'm truly sorry. I feel really guilty when I treat you like this after all you've done for me. I guess I use you as my whipping boy. My mom and dad have so many problems already. I can't shout at them, or the hospital staff. I've just gotta scream at somebody. Forgive me."

Jackie smiled warmly. "What are friends for, Joni?" She meant it.

Friends like Dick and Jackie continued their ministry with visits of hope and words from the Bible.

"God's only allowing your trials for a purpose, to teach you endurance and strengthen your faith," Dick told her one day.

It was the encouragement of words and actions that enabled Joni to arrive at a more positive attitude toward her disablement. She would later admit that even with her new attitude, her ups and downs were very much like the pattern of her temperature chart hanging by her bed.

If it was hard for most normal teenagers to sail through that stage of their life on an even keel, it was much more difficult for Joni. Without any preparation, without warning, straight from being an embodiment of Action Woman, she had been suddenly pinioned on a canvas frame, to be turned over like a chicken on a spit every two hours. She was only capable of movement and feeling from her shoulders to the crown of her head. How could she express herself or get rid of her frustrations? Her ups and downs were to be expected.

In spite of her changing moods, she was still able to count her blessings. Looking back on the situation, Joni later wrote, "I most appreciated people who came armed with love . . . and magazines and doughnuts . . . those helping me write letters or bringing writing paper and envelopes—even stamps . . . I especially remember a few girls who made it a weekly ritual to come by and do my nails."

Dick's last present before leaving for college was a large-print Bible on which she could focus while she hung suspended over the floor. All she needed was a friend to turn the pages at regular intervals.

Joni was grateful for those simple acts of kindness by her friends. They made all the difference.

Such kindness made the following months that much harder to bear when people, one by one, began to drift away or move on to other parts of their lives. The old crowd of friends, of which she had been the center, were spreading their wings with jobs and plans for college. Joni was left behind, unable to fulfil any of her ambitions.

Her relationship with Dick was the hardest. He was a devoted friend, but his plans and Joni's possessiveness made the change difficult. She hated herself for it. She could hear herself nagging him on his visits to the hospital, even though she knew it was a sacrifice for him to be there. He had to hitchhike his way to the hospital and would give up valuable study time in order to do so.

"You're late, Dickie, . . . Tell me you love me."

The need for his love and the frustration over not having her needs met all the time left her feeling that she would certainly ruin the relationship.

Joni's hospital bill was mounting daily and she sensed the strain it put on her parents. So when the hospital therapist stopped by the next day to make plans for rehabilitation, Joni was excited. It was her chance to make a positive contribution to her own recovery. *Boy! Will I show them!* "I'll give it everything I've got," she told the therapist. It was just as well that she couldn't see the struggle ahead.

"Your fracture was at the fourth and fifth cervical level. We're going to try to train your other muscles in the back and shoulders to do the work of the arm muscles that are out of action. This is normal procedure for patients with your sorts of injuries."

The therapy began with Joni's arms fastened in slings. She put every ounce of energy into her attempts to make her arms move. It had been a movement taken for granted before, but now she was only able to raise her arm an inch twice during the first half-hour session.

She begged for a rest. Her instructor was encouraging despite Joni's obvious disappointment.

"Good try, Joni. Don't worry too much," she smiled at the end of the session. "I'll be working with you every day until you're ready for Greenoaks."

"Where's that?!" Joni asked with excitement.

"It's a super rehabilitation center that specializes in cases like yours. Dr. Sherill will tell you more about it. As soon as they have a place ready for you, we'll pass you on to them. Chin up, Joni, it's the next step in your recovery program."

Joni beamed happily. "Great! That's where I'll learn to walk."

She needed the boost to her spirits. From that point on she concentrated all her energies into getting her remaining muscles to work. Those efforts, though they did not lead to her desired goal, did help her in the long run.

The anticipated day for Joni's move to Greenoaks arrived with a flurry of activity and farewells from the staff. Nurses popped in one by one to wish her well. When Joni promised Dr. Harris that she would come back one day on her own two feet, he didn't contradict her but simply laughed and kidded with her. He was wise enough to know that a wet blanket of reality was not needed at that point.

The gifts and memorabilia Joni had accumulated during the three and a half months in the hospital ward were piled into boxes. And then Joni herself was placed on a gurney and wheeled out of the hospital into an ambulance for her trip to Greenoaks.

The scene outside the hospital was quite a contrast with the scene when she first entered in July. Then it had been hot with trees in full leaf and flower beds brimming with color. Now the fresh autumn air and the reddish tints of the leaves accompanied her to the next phase of her life.

Just as there was a contrast in the weather between her entry and exit from the hospital, there was also a contrast in Joni's expectations. Upon entering the hospital she wondered how long it would be until she was cured. Now she felt a cure would be closer, though not without some patience being required. She was optimistic and ready for the next stage. Life wasn't too bad, after all!

Greenoaks, here I come! she exulted silently.

———

It was unfortunate that she had built up a wonderful mental picture of the place. Instead of the stately home she had expected, Greenoaks looked for all the world like an ordinary factory or office building. Her dream was quickly tarnished.

The inside of the building fared no better. Most of the

shabby rooms needed a face-lift and some paint. All the patients were anchored in frames, beds, or wheelchairs instead of hobbling around under their own power. Joni's vision of a place where paralyzed people were cured was not just tarnished, it was destroyed.

Joni's parents tried to make the best of the situation and put on a good front for Joni, but they too were disappointed.

The attitude of one of Joni's new roommates did not make the transition any easier.

Anne met Joni's arrival with a string of verbal invectives. Anne had remembered Joni from the hospital as the patient who had been held up to the others as a model of what a patient should be like. Fortunately, the other three patients were fun to be with and were eager to include Joni in their group.

Joni could excuse Anne for polluting the ward with cigarette smoke and hurting other people with bitter and cutting remarks. Joni sensed that behind that facade of hostility was a very lonely person, frightened and longing for an easy death to end it all.

I know just how she feels, thought Joni. She remembered how she had begged Jackie to help her commit suicide. That made her all the more determined to persevere with overtures of friendship. She refused to be put off by the many rebuffs Anne gave her. This would be a make-or-break situation for Joni, and it gave her a worthwhile project to occupy her thoughts. Joni needed the distraction.

The transfer to Greenoaks did not prove to be exhilarating. Instead, life settled down into a rather boring routine of eating, sleeping, and television. The overworked staff was stretched to the limit to complete just the ordinary chores. Friends were restricted to the visiting hours as established by Greenoaks. There was no relaxing of the rules under any circumstances.

Sister Jay made a breakthrough one day in the facility's vision of what a visitor should do.

She became an active participant in helping Joni. A new crop of peach fuzz had begun to grow on Joni's scalp, and so Jay became an accomplished hairdresser. Joni's roommates soon looked forward to Jay's visits, as they too became free clients of Jay's service. It encouraged them greatly to get their hair washed so often.

Joni's long stay in the hospital and Greenoaks began to have an effect on her bones and skin. Her bones were pushing through her skin and causing bedsores. Worse yet was the lack of any progress made in her recovery.

Joni argued with her therapists. "What's the use of all this exercising? I've made no progress. I still can't feel a thing." Undaunted by Joni's criticism, the therapists continued their work and their encouragement.

"Never mind. It's all for a purpose. We've got to keep your muscles supple. Otherwise your circulation would create lots of problems," they told her.

As pointless as the exercises seemed, it was the tilting of Joni's body from a prone position to an upright position that concerned her most. Tilted one degree at a time, Joni's body had to get used to the new way in which it would have to circulate blood—especially to the brain.

"Hold it! I can't take any more. My head is swimming," she wailed.

"Don't worry," they told her. "Your heart will soon get back to normal. We'll do it a little bit at a time."

Joni's friend Diana proved to be a pillar of strength as the therapy regimen increased. She shared Joni's excitement at the slightest progress. She shared Bible verses regularly with Joni to comfort and encourage her. Her optimism was infectious. Joni's outlook brightened daily through Diana's ministry.

————

Joni greeted Diana's entrance excitedly one day. "Hey! What do you think? Our church is organizing an all-night prayer vigil for my healing and recovery."

"That's really great, Joni. Particularly now that you're getting some sensation back into your fingers. It could be the start of better times."

Joni went to bed that night convinced that she would jump out of bed the next morning, fully healed.

Though the prayer meeting took place, the desired healing did not. Undaunted, she told her friends and family, "Don't worry, the Lord's going to do it in His own time."

Inwardly, Joni seethed with frustration. *How much longer will I have to wait?* she wondered. Dick might have been right about "all things working together for good," but there were too many times when she found it hard to relate that truth to her own situation.

Joni was refreshingly honest as she wrote about her reactions. She didn't disguise her reactions or try to make out that she bore all her sufferings with saintly composure. Such honesty has proven to be a vital factor in her ministry with millions of people, disabled and able-bodied. Her honesty has allowed her to identify with people's suffering, and her joy has encouraged people with illnesses to see how they can accept their situation.

In her book *Seeking God,* Joni described her feelings about her time in Greenoaks.

"The toughest part of those early days . . . was living up to my reputation as a Christian when people came to visit me. I felt as if people expected me to put on a happy face. Try as I might, I just couldn't. My failure made me feel even more guilty about letting down my parents, my pastor, and my Christian friends."

God was watching, however, and knew Joni's heart. He did not expect Joni to try to put on a front for people. He alone knew her innermost feelings and that someday even those feelings would work together for good and bring Him glory.

5

*I*t was Christmas before Joni would take her next car ride. Propped up in the seat of her parents' automobile, fully dressed in her own clothes rather than a drab hospital gown, Joni was on her way home past a snowy landscape to celebrate the holidays. Jay had even given Joni a blond wig to cover the new crop of short hair.

The outing was for just one day to celebrate Christmas at home, but her mother spared no effort in making Joni feel comfortable. She was able to procure a hospital bed which she placed on one side of the dining room so that Joni could be a part of all the festivities. She could not explore the rest of the house, but she could enjoy meals with the family and look into the living room. Being at home brought back a flood of memories.

Despite the festivities and the opportunity to be out of Greenoaks for a day, Joni's feelings were mixed. She felt self-conscious about her deformity and begged her mother to tuck a rug over her useless legs. She couldn't help but notice the contrast between her lifeless body and the beautiful decorations and atmosphere surrounding Christmas day.

Dick and other friends called on her that day. She was grateful for all the love and care lavished on her and wished Christmas could last forever.

But she was glad when at the end of the day she was returned to the hospital ward. There she could give vent to her tears that she struggled to keep back while she was with family and friends. It was just as well that she had not been able to make a tour of the entire house, especially her bedroom. Being there would have brought back too many memories.

Her desire to be back on the ward seemed a little too prophetic. She soon found out that her Christmas-day adventure would be the last for a very long time. She would be grounded for more surgery.

"Hard luck, Joni. We hate to do this to you just when you'd made some improvement," the nurse said. "The fact is your bone projections are rubbing the skin on your back and hips. Your only chance of healing them is to go back on the Stryker Frame."

Deep despondency set in again. It seemed unbearably cruel not to be allowed to sit up even for short intervals after she had struggled so hard to get to that point. It would mean starting all over again.

Thoughts of suicide returned.

There's no future for me and I can't cling to Dick forever. It's just not fair to him. If the only part of my body I can move is my head, I'll never be capable of leading an independent life. In fact, I'm little better than a vegetable, she thought to herself.

She underwent a long operation without anesthesia to grind down the protruding bones on her hips and tailbone. Recovery from the operation did not go well, and she was put back on the Stryker Frame again. The wounds had burst open a second time.

The same thoughts she fought earlier in her hospitalization came back. This time family problems added to the despair. Her sister Jay's divorce had become final. Joni grieved for her and her daughter, Kay. Jay tried not to worry Joni with the break-up of her marriage, but Joni sensed the sadness behind the facade Jay put on.

But in spite of her own pain, Jay had a wonderful proposal.

"Kay and I would love for you to come and live with us when you're finally discharged. You'd be company for both of us."

It cheered Joni to think that at least one person believed she could someday lead a more normal existence—mixing with other people instead of only doctors, nurses, and patients.

Though the thought of a normal life encouraged Joni, she was not yet ready to take steps to get there. When Chris, her therapist, suggested one day that she might try to paint with a brush in her mouth or type with a mouth-controlled stick, Joni became adamant in her rejection.

"No way, Chris. I think it's a perfectly disgusting idea."

It was not so much the picture of doing things with her mouth that repulsed Joni but rather the fact that learning such a technique meant she would give up hope of ever using her hands again. The faint tingling she had felt before gave her hope that perhaps she could regain use of them with therapy.

Being confronted with the future included not only physical choices but relational ones as well. Her relationship with Dick was subtly changing. Without openly discussing it, both had come to the conclusion that marriage, if at all possible, was not probable for a very long time.

Despite this realization, Dick never let Joni down. As long as he was around, he came in regularly to offer friendship and support. Joni agreed mentally with the Scripture messages he pointed out to her because of his devotion. But afterwards, she was more honest with herself.

That's okay for a guy who's physically fit, but what does it do for me, lashed on to my Stryker? I need something more relevant to my situation.

Joni's friend Diana served to meet that need in Joni's life with not only words from Scripture but with her life as well. She read from the Old Testament prophets, particularly Jeremiah.

"Now that's what I call real suffering," mused Joni. "I can begin to identify with what he's saying about deep, inward hurt. I've thought that myself."

Though in tune with someone like Jeremiah, the daily dose of Bible verses from Dick and Diana did not always help.

"I can't take it from you," she said to them. "They're just too glib, trite, and superficial."

Joni's state of mind was not helped by some of the treatment she received by the staff. One of the attendants was deliberately cruel and offensive to her when no one was looking, blackmailing Joni afterwards to keep her quiet. Many of the other assistants did not set out to ill-treat her, but the level of their care for her suffered because they were poorly paid and were given far to many duties to get through in time. Her faith reached an all-time low.

Strangely enough, her struggle with faith came at an unusual time. A young quadriplegic named Jim Pollard entered her life—not as a romantic interest—but as a sparring partner with regards to belief in God. He could not hold his head up, but his piercing questions as an atheist shook Joni to the core.

"Religion's merely shallow. The idea of a personal God is absolutely ridiculous. Get the most you can out of life now—there's certainly no afterlife," was the premise of his entire argument with Joni.

Laid out in a ward with other patients made his words

sound more convincing. He added more fuel to his argument with convincing books and pamphlets on agnosticism. Joni's thoughts of influencing Jim for Christ vanished under the weight of the arguments. She became confused.

Despite her confusion, one thing was still clear in her mind. She had found out toward the end of her senior year of high school that merely temporal and secular things were unable to satisfy her completely. She didn't accept a purely materialistic view of life.

"Give me time, Jim. I'm still trying to sort it all out," she told him.

"There's no God, Joni, and no future existence. You've just got to live for the here and now. I'm telling you."

Joni grew frightened. Reading Jim's choice of literature made it easy to be influenced to deny God. In desperation she prayed, "I've come to the end of the road. I've got to admit it. If you don't exist, there's no point in carrying on. It's all up to you now, Lord, to prove to me that you really are there."

Being a fair-minded person, Joni still persevered in reading widely. She was determined to examine all the evidence before coming to a final decision. Yet the more she delved into atheistic writings, the more muddled, unsure, and unhappy she became. Finally, she turned back to the Bible, convinced that God was real but that there was no way she could understand His dealings with her.

One ray of encouragement pierced the gloom during that difficult period. Diana announced one day she was going to become a volunteer worker at the facility so that she could spend more time with Joni.

Joni was torn in two directions. It would be great to have such a good friend close at hand when most of the other staff was stretched already, but . . .

"Diana, I appreciate your thoughtfulness, but I don't

like you dropping out of college for my sake."

"I've made up my mind. It will only be for a couple of terms or so until God gives me guidance about my career."

Joni was not the only one who benefitted from Diana's decision. Other patients enjoyed her spirit and willingness to help. And Joni had an able counselor on hand to talk about things that concerned her.

"I'm scared, Diana," Joni confessed to her one day. "I haven't the faintest idea what's going to happen to me in the future. It's all too vague."

"Guess it all boils down to trusting the Lord," Diana answered. "He doesn't always let us know all the answers a long time ahead. How about you trying something more positive for a change instead of probing the past?"

"Such as. . . ?"

"Such as trying occupational therapy as a challenge. Your therapist is sure you could write and draw with pens in your mouth. Why don't you have a shot at it? There's nothing lost in having a go."

Oh, dear, thought Joni. Was that admitting defeat? She still nursed a secret hope that she would one day regain the use of her hands. Still, it made sense in the meantime to make an effort, even if it was only to help pass the time more quickly. She would at least try it out.

The occupational therapist, Chris, was delighted with Joni's decision. She made the experience as meaningful as she could, but the process of learning to write and paint with her mouth was not a pleasant one for Joni. It began with a few wobbly lines and squiggles, but Joni persevered and the jagged symbols soon became letters. Letters turned into words and eventually she managed to write her first full-page letter home to her parents. It was a small but significant milestone on her road to recovery.

One last operation on her protruding bones and two

weeks face down on the Stryker Frame gave Joni time to read several Christian books, including C.S. Lewis' *Mere Christianity*. Her mother sat for hours turning the pages.

Joni's birthday, October 15, marked a special occasion. The skin on her back had healed, and she was flipped on her back again so that she could greet friends and family that came to visit.

The day marked the beginning of a new era. It was "the clear shining after rain" that had eluded Joni for so long. Prospects were good that she would soon be able to move around in a wheelchair, giving her the independence she desired. She had watched other patients at Greenoaks earn their independence in such a way and she knew her day would come.

Joni's renewed hope led her to experiment with other forms of therapy. She painted ceramic disks and then sketched with a sharp stylus on wet clay.

Chris, her therapist, was delighted with Joni's progress and attitude. "That's fantastic. You've got real skill. We'll work at it together."

"Well, I used to enjoy sketching when I had the use of my hands, Chris."

"So your talent is there already. Hands are only a tool. You're going to use a new tool, your mouth, from now on."

6

Although Joni's body did not experience healing, her mind was renewed daily. She no longer seethed with rebellion and anger. She still could not see how her life could work together for good, but time passed pleasantly and quickly. Her faith strengthened more and more each day.

Joni's artwork improved day by day as well. She progressed to sketching with soft charcoal pencils on drawing paper and was amazed at her own success. She found a way to express her creativity, which she had assumed would never find expression after the accident. She no longer felt like a vegetable.

Her growing faith and improving talent combined in every drawing. Underneath each signature she penned the letters PTL.

When asked years later what that meant by a newspaper reporter, Joni said, "It stands for Praise The Lord. You see . . . God loves us—He does care. For those who love God, everything—even what happened to me at age seventeen—works together for good. . . . My art is a reflection of how God can empower someone like me to rise above circumstances."

Joni's art gave her an opportunity to be a giver, and not merely a receiver, of love. She made presents for her friends who had so thoughtfully brought little gifts to cheer her up. She was able to store up a secret hoard of Christmas presents for her family. That Christmas would be a far better one than the one-day visit she had the previous Christmas. She worked feverishly at the drawing pad.

Achieving her goal was not easy. Joni had to regain lost ground as a result of the two operations to shave her bones. The therapist put her through the various stages of therapy in order to sit up again. She then moved on to exercises to develop control over various movements. A lightly fit corset was also used to support the upper part of her body.

Joni's parents picked her up at Greenoaks on Christmas Eve. With her hair freshly styled and an attractive new outfit that fit her well, Joni traveled home in an upbeat frame of mind.

Christmas that year was indeed much better than the last. She no longer had the same fears. She felt more physically fit and her outlook on life was much more optimistic. Although she expected more disappointments ahead, her maturity as a Christian gave her a new sense of confidence.

No amount of optimism could have prepared Joni for the best present she would receive that Christmas. Her parents gave it to her in the form of a proposal. "Joni, how do you feel about transferring to a new hospital in California? It's in Los Angeles and they're getting some remarkable results. A few really hopeless cases have been taught to use their arms and legs again." Joni's parents had investigated the possibility and had made application on Joni's behalf. She would have to wait until a room opened up.

"That sounds wonderful!" Joni agreed. "It would be the best thing that could possibly happen to me. Let's pray it will work out."

A portion of the Christmas holiday was spent with Dick. They even went to the cinema one evening. While it was refreshing to be with each other outside of a hospital room, there was an awkwardness and distance between them. Joni longed for the natural, carefree relationship to be established again and wondered when that might happen.

She also wondered about going back to Greenoaks. Being at home made her realize just how much she did not enjoy Greenoaks. She resented having to go back.

"Stop worrying, Joni," her father told her one day. "There will be no need to go back. We've just had a call from the rehabilitation center in California. They have a spare bed for you. We'll fly out there together."

Joni's prayers were answered as she had hoped and she responded enthusiastically.

"I just can't wait!"

The wait was not hard for Joni. The days fled by with more celebrations and the old familiar customs. And the prospect of regaining use of her hands at the new rehabilitation center occupied her thoughts during quiet hours.

The flight to Los Angeles was exciting for Joni. She had never flown before and when they landed, the weather was sunny and balmy, a welcome contrast to the freezing cold temperatures they'd left behind in Baltimore.

Joni had not allowed herself to create an unrealistic picture of her new home. She wanted to avoid the disappointment she had felt when she moved to Greenoaks. She need not have done so.

The staff at the new facility was much younger and not overworked. There were less rules, and visits from friends were not regarded as an unwelcome interruption. In fact, they were positively encouraged. Joni's mood became buoyant and even more optimistic.

Though her parents could not stay in California, Jay and

her daughter Kay rented an apartment nearby. It felt great to have some family so close when she was three thousand miles away from home.

———

Joni's rehabilitation began in earnest very quickly after moving to Los Angeles. She worked hard to replace her arm muscles with those of her upper back and shoulders. Her first task was to learn how to feed herself.

Using a bent spoon attached to a leather arm brace, Joni learned the skill of forcing food onto the spoon and up to the mouth. It required enormous concentration, and the first attempts left a lot of messy food on the table. Fortunately, her inability to feed herself for the past year and a half drove Joni to keep at it. She soon perfected the technique.

Having learned to feed herself, Joni's next objective was to learn how to get around in a wheelchair on her own. Her first attempts after being strapped into a chair were pitiful. She moved only thirty feet in the first two hours!

But just as the thought of feeding herself spurred Joni on to use the spoon, her desire to move about independently also inspired her to persevere with the wheelchair. Soon she was fitted for an electric wheelchair and a new world opened up to her.

With the doctor's promise that she would be discharged just four months after her arrival, Joni relished the new world. She wasn't content to travel at a slow, sedate pace. She became more daring instead.

"Let's race right around the corridors to the front door!" challenged Rick, another quadriplegic.

"Okay. You're on! Let the best man win!"

Unfortunately, the race ended in a minor catastrophe as Joni crashed into a nurse carrying a tray full of bottles and jugs. Joni had shouted a warning but couldn't stop herself in time. The accident resulted in Joni losing use of her wheelchair as punishment. Wheelchairs were not toys, and policy had to be observed if residents were going to be out on their own someday.

———————

Rehabilitation completed, the day arrived for Joni's release.

"What about my hands, Doctor?" she asked before leaving.

"Just forget about them, Joni. They'll never be any use. Try and be reconciled to the idea. Count your other blessings."

It was not the news Joni wanted or expected. She had come to California with great hopes, and though she had learned a lot, it was a setback to be told that her hands were beyond rehabilitation.

Upon returning to Maryland, her immediate thoughts focused on her relationship with Dick. She had longed for the day when she could be released from the hospital and get married. But she realized she could not saddle Dick with a helpless wife. She loved him too much to let him undertake such a burden.

Tearfully she wrote to Dick.

"God hasn't answered our prayers. I'll never be able to use my hands again. Marriage would be out of the question . . . I hope we shall always continue to be special friends."

In the midst of her sadness she added, "But do date other girls and pray that God will lead you to the right person in the end. You have my blessing."

It was a costly sacrifice for Joni. She had given up a really precious relationship that had meant a great deal to her, but she could see no other alternative. It seemed unlikely that any man would come into her life again to enrich it as Dick had done. The separation was a bitter pill to swallow, but she knew it was the right thing to do.

Breaking off the relationship was symbolic of the breaking away she had done from the rehabilitation center. Joni had made remarkable progress while at the center. The staff had worked hard to achieve that, but there was nothing new left to be done. From that point on it was a case of maintaining and improving the skills she had acquired. She was on her own.

Moving back to Maryland was good for Joni. She could be with her family without the restriction of visiting hours. And she would need to be there, as she would soon enter another period of depression. She confessed later in *All God's Children,* "Only weeks out of the hospital, I spent most of my time by the dining room window staring at fallen leaves. They swirled gracefully in circles. I envied those leaves, for they could move. I couldn't."

Perhaps the finality of her immobility struck her the hardest. Perhaps she had fooled herself into thinking that she could do more or that she would be healed. Whatever the expectations she had created, the realization that life was not going to be much different made it difficult.

And hers was not the only tragedy that made the days so depressing. Not only had Jay's divorce been hard on the family, but they learned that a niece, Kelly, was dying of brain cancer. *When is it going to all end?*

Questioning her father one day, Joni found him to be refreshingly frank. "I don't reckon to know all the answers yet, honey, but I'm sure God has everything under control. He knows what He's doing to us and it's not just for spite."

Although it helped to share her worries with her father, it failed to lift her out of her depression completely. To deal with it, Joni repeatedly indulged in wild daydreams and fantasies—anything to escape from the harsh world of reality. She found herself living in the past mentally, feeding her mind on former pleasures and almost sensual experiences.

Outwardly she took good care to appear the same cheerful Joni who was bravely trying to come to terms with her paralysis while inwardly she was raging against God.

It was her friend Diana who noticed the battle. She had come to live with the Eareckson family during the summer. Diana didn't suspect anything was wrong at first. It seemed natural that Joni was more subdued and less of an extrovert than before her accident.

But as the days passed, Diana's close relationship with Joni allowed her to notice Joni's silent retreats into the past. And she knew that it was unhealthy. Far from indicating a mind that was calmly sorting out her problems, it suggested that Joni's state of mind was deteriorating.

Diana could not dole out sympathy. As much as she felt sorry for her friend, she could not let the dreaming continue.

"Wake up, Joni!" she said one day. "You've got to forget about the past and live in the present."

Joni didn't take her friend's advice immediately. She was annoyed at her friend's interference but eventually understood that she wasn't doing herself any good by living in her strange dream world. And she was sinning against God.

In desperation, she turned to Him in prayer.

"I know you've got a plan for my future, but I need outside help to discover what your will is for me. Please intervene in my life to teach me and guide me."

She had prayed that prayer once before and His answer took her into the world of disability, depression, and loss. *What will He do this time?*

7

*D*iana provided God's answer.

"Tell you what, Joni," she announced suddenly one day. "I'm thinking of asking a friend of mine over to meet you. His name's Steve Estes. I think you'll get on well with him."

Although Joni had returned to Maryland with great mobility and independence, Diana could see that Joni was struggling to work out answers for herself. A newcomer to the scene would provide a fresh approach to the problem.

Joni's first response wasn't overly enthusiastic, particularly when she learned how young he was.

"A guy still in high school? What can he do for me?"

"Give him a chance, Joni. I'm sure you'll like him when you meet him. For a youngster, he's a very mature Christian."

Diana's reply was prophetic, though even she could not have imagined just how well Joni and Steve would get along. Their friendship would last for many years.

Steve Estes was a tall and lanky sixteen-year-old. He was not gifted as many boys his age in things like athletics, but he had the special gift of knowing and teaching God's Word. That gift, combined with his honest and down-to-earth approach to Joni, made for many hours of growth for her.

Steve approached Joni as an ordinary teenager and not a "patient."

Joni observed later, "I liked this young Christian man because he always brought me Dunkin' Donuts or pizza or R.C. colas. So whenever he opened his Bible, I listened.

"This boy, Steve Estes, used his gift to start me searching through Scripture and on to a life of meaning and hope."

Joni wasn't always enthused about his lessons. Steve needed to use shock therapy on occasion to get to the core of Joni's problem very quickly.

"Joni," he said one day. "What about giving thanks, even though you're in a wheelchair?"

Joni was startled. "Steve, I can't. I'd feel like a hypocrite and that's the last thing I'd want to be."

"Well, wait a minute. It does say, 'Give thanks in all circumstances, for this is God's will for you in Christ Jesus.' You may not feel great or understand why God is putting you through all this suffering. It's not a question of waiting until all the conditions are right. You just have to trust God."

The concept caught Joni off guard, but she had to admit that it seemed to make sense and that it was obviously God's Word. She trusted what Steve showed her.

In a quiet time of honest submission she told God how difficult she found it to thank Him.

"But I am grateful for the progress I'm making with my therapy."

It would be a long time before exuberant praise and thanksgiving became a part of Joni's life, but it was that first step with Steve as her coach that it was possible at all.

Steve had no prior experience with disabled people but he was always eager to help. He was clumsy and felt awkward at times, but because they were both in a learning situation, Joni felt at ease. Neither one dominated the other.

"God used the long hours he and I shared over an open Bible to lift my spirits and turn my thinking around . . . you'd think God would have brought my way some smartly dressed, good-looking youth director to grab my attention and get me into God's Word. But no . . . the Lord had me spend time with another kid my age—a young boy with the spiritual gift of teaching."

Steve also learned from the experience. "As a friend, he learned how to hold a glass of soda to my mouth, push my wheelchair, or empty my legbag."

Steve and Joni's relationship would be mutually supportive for many years to come, and the lessons he learned in helping Joni would be invaluable when he would later become a pastor. The two have always kept in touch and collaborated on Joni's second book, *A Step Further*.

While the exchange during those first weeks would seem uneven to many, the lessons Steve learned would help to expand his ministry to others. He tentatively suggested to Joni that they start a Bible study at her house every Wednesday evening and include others.

Joni was excited about the idea and Diana was the first recruit.

"Count me in too, please, Steve, and I'm sure Jay and some others would like to be included. Is that okay with you?"

"Sure, the more the merrier. Let's see how it works out," Steve said.

The Bible study soon became the highlight of the week for everyone. Joni, in particular, found herself growing in knowledge and understanding. She began to look at life from God's viewpoint instead of being engrossed in her problems. She saw the value of the Bible as a daily guide-book for living and realized she had been playing with fire in her relationships before the accident.

The Bible showed Joni that God had a very good reason for all His commands and prohibitions. He wasn't being a kill-joy in stipulating no sex before marriage. It was an essential rule to ensure the happiness and welfare of young people. Realizing the love behind God's plan, she was thankful that she had cooled her friendship with Jason before it was too late!

Steve sensed as he led the study that it was more than issues concerning lifestyle about which the young people needed to know. They also needed to know the basic truths about God and His Son. He took the truths and explained them in simple terms and made it a point to challenge the young people to practice the truths.

"You need to put it into practical use, not just tell people about it."

Joni's spiritual life began to grow steadily. It no longer looked like a graph of high peaks and low valleys. Looking outside herself, she began to appreciate how other people also suffered—people like Job, Paul, and Jeremiah. In the end, although the process was far from easy, they had triumphed through God's grace.

Joni also found it helpful to commit Bible passages to memory. She brought them to mind to comfort her when she would go through a bad spell emotionally. Doing so kept her from escaping to dreams and fantasies.

I must live in the present now, she decided. *It's useless to keep dwelling on the past.* To show that she really meant business with God, she gave away her lacrosse and hockey sticks that had meant so much to her before. The greatest sacrifice of all was to sell her beloved Tumbleweed. The horse had given her many hours of pleasure. ". . . I loved riding. I used to train horses to jump and often entered them in horse shows around Maryland and Pennsylvania."

Giving up her best treasures took her to places where God would be her only resource. In *Seeking God,* Joni cites Abraham Lincoln in order to capture her thoughts at the times of such sacrifice:

"I have been driven many times to my knees by the overwhelming conviction that I had nowhere else to go."

All of Joni's props that made her popular or gave her enjoyment and meaning had been taken away. Although there had been nothing wrong with the pursuits, there was no future in them for Joni after her accident. The time for useless regrets had passed.

Joni's father gave her good advice as she let go of these things and as she wrestled with the fact that she could not use her hands creatively as she once had.

"You're doing something much more important. You're building character and you don't need hands to do that."

———

As Joni began to build her character in conformity with what she was learning with Steve, God began opening new windows to see how He was working.

She began counting her blessings. She was out of the hospital, her family was supportive, her friend Diana had put her life on hold for her, and a new friend, Steve, had entered her life. She also counted as blessings some of the more difficult circumstances in her life. Giving up Dick was one such circumstance.

It had cost Joni dearly to end her relationship with Dick.

He was supportive and accepting of her condition. He had told her months before, "God only gives good gifts, so I look on you and your handicap as a special blessing."

Despite such acceptance, Joni could see that such a viewpoint alone could not serve as a realistic basis for a relationship. God confirmed that decision in a special way.

By unselfishly releasing him from his commitment to her, she retained his friendship as well as enlarging her circle of friends. As Dick began to date other girls, he would often bring them by Joni's house to introduce them. The pain of ending their commitment to each other brought new friendships for Joni and Dick.

Joni remained confined to the house the rest of the year. She longed for the time when she would be able to get out and travel, but God saw fit to keep her close to home. (Little did she know that traveling would become a regular routine in her later years!)

Being in the midst of a supportive family made the confinement easier, as did the help of friends and neighbors. She was touched by the spontaneous offers of help from such people.

"Neighbors would often call my mother and say, 'Look, I'm on my way to the market. Have your list ready, and I'll be glad to pick up your items,' " Joni recalled. And practical measures of help continued during those days at home. Her mom did not need to send out an SOS. People were sensitive to the situation and rallied around.

Diana returned to college in the fall to study psychology but still lived with Joni's family. The two would often try out psychology experiments on each other that Diana had learned in class that day. One night Joni was lifted onto the couch, changing places with Diana who sat in Joni's chair.

Joni felt very relaxed, but Diana felt as though the wheel-chair created a gulf between her and other people.

Such experiments helped Diana and other friends to learn new ways of expressing their friendship with Joni.

Joni has often observed, "I guess it's a barrier (the wheelchair)—it makes folks behave awkwardly when they come up and talk to me. Some even think I must be mentally handicapped as well."

Joni's friends took such observations to heart. Whenever Diana and the others went out, for example, they would casually walk beside Joni rather than behind her as if she were a patient being wheeled down a hospital hallway.

On such occasions Joni had to put up with the stares of people. They were not pleasant, but it seemed an inevitable part of the treatment that disabled people receive. Such behavior was not meant to be offensive. Most people acted out of ignorance. As she would later lead seminars on the subject, Joni taught people the need to treat disabled people as normally as possible.

"People who stare . . . are forgetting that the disabled person has real feelings and needs. Try a warm smile or initiate friendly conversation."

Lessons weren't only to be learned by Joni's able-bodied friends. Diana's psychology experiments in role playing pointed out things Joni had not considered before. Seeing Diana act in a demanding way while in a wheelchair taught Joni that she was being overly demanding at times and expecting people to respond to her immediately.

It was humbling but Joni got the point.

"Gee, I'm really sorry," she remarked. "I'll try to be more considerate with you guys in the future."

Joni's relationship with her friends continued to grow in an honest and challenging way. It prepared her well for the ministry and message of friendship she would communicate in years to come.

8

*T*he more Steve showed God's will from the Bible, the more Joni became convinced that God had sent Steve into her life as an answer to her desperate prayer for change. Joni was not just learning facts about God and the Bible; she learned to apply the truth to her own circumstances so that it became an active and living thing.

"Steve, I believe that even this old chair can become a tool rather than remain a tragedy, though I can't see just how at the moment," she confided to him one day.

God's living Word sparked in her a longing to make a contribution to society. She was tired of merely being on the receiving end. In time she felt less sensitive and awkward as she ventured out in public. She threw herself into the exploration of God's creation, something she had missed for almost two years of her life.

Joni was put to use right away in her desire to contribute something. Steve asked her to give a brief chat one evening to the other teenagers at his church youth club. Though she accepted the challenge in faith, Joni felt petrified and tongue-tied.

She had reason to feel that way. The talk was not a good experience. A few awkward phrases came out as she related her feelings surrounding her accident until she eventually dried up. Red-faced and stuttering, she wished the earth would swallow her up. Steve had to step in and pick up the pieces of her thoughts and put them together for the kids in the audience.

"I'll never be articulate, Steve," she moaned. "That's the end of that little experiment. Don't put me through that again."

"C'mon on, Joni, don't be disheartened," he comforted her. "It's only to be expected. You're not the only one. I reacted in the same way myself. With more practice and a little training, you'll make it. You should go to college in your wheelchair."

The thought of college intrigued Joni. Her brain had grown a little rusty after such a long time away from school. But she wondered if she would be up to the challenge. It seemed like a frightening prospect.

Steve reassured her.

"There are quite a few disabled students at the University of Maryland. The staff are used to people with handicaps."

"Well, maybe I should give it a try. But I can't do it all on my own. I'll need some help from Jay and Diana."

Joni had always been quick to acknowledge that it takes supporters to get any task done. She paid tribute to them in her book *All God's Children* and especially to the team that kept her going when she enrolled in the fall for a course in public speaking.

"I never dared to dream of going to college. . . . There were just too many obstacles to overcome. Thankfully, another friend arranged my transportation to and from campus . . . [I needed] volunteers to assist with note-taking, and students to escort me from one class to the next. I even needed someone to feed me at the school cafeteria."

Fortunately, there was never any shortage of volunteers to share the different duties. Jay and Diana were regular helpers.

Helpers were not the only contacts she made. She soon found other people in wheelchairs. Such contacts allowed her to grasp, albeit dimly at first, a little of the kind of service God planned for her future. She would be involved in the lives of other disabled people, she knew, but she had no idea of the magnitude of impact that such a desire would have.

Attending college gave Joni further encouragement not to look back to the past. It also took her mind off her current physical limitations. She was forced to look ahead.

————————

In February of 1970, Joni shared a painful experience with her family. Her five-year-old niece, Kelly, died of a brain tumor. Kelly had been in pain for over a year and the family was grateful for her release, but the loss was heavy. It left a painful gap in their family circle, which had recently lost Kelly's father to divorce. That left Linda, her mom, with two boys to support alone.

Joni's response to losing Kelly was different than at other times. She had learned by this time that it was not necessary nor helpful to look for reasons why God had allowed Kelly to die. Posing such a question would only lead to frustration and unhappiness. Blind trust in God was the only alternative. In His time He would reveal more.

Joni accepted Kelly's death well, but it was nice to have Steve's support through this period. He encouraged her with passages from the Bible to help her focus on what God might have in mind for her as a result of the suffering she had experienced.

"Joni, isn't it exciting to think that God might use your sufferings in the same way as Paul's, 'For the advantage of the gospel'? [Philippians 1:12] He's letting you suffer on His behalf."

Acknowledgement of this truth was not readily apparent. Joni still struggled with thankfulness for her current situation. She had learned to accept it and trust God, but she had not yet learned to thank Him. Such thankfulness would be necessary in order for her to be used effectively.

Her thoughts were hopeful and honest.

"Oh dear! I don't always feel like giving thanks when it's something unpleasant. Well! I guess I ought to get into the habit of giving thanks. Maybe in time my thankfulness will be genuine."

Obedience to the command to be thankful led to another lesson from God. Steve led the lesson.

"Joni," he startled her one day. "I guess you've got a poor self-image. What are you going to do about it?"

"Why should I, Steve? What's wrong with that?"

"Well, you put a low value on yourself—perhaps because you're always looking at your own shortcomings. God appreciates you for your own worth. After all, you're His creation—so it doesn't matter too much what other peoples' opinions are."

Joni responded positively to Steve's encouragement. She wondered if there might even be hidden gifts in her that she hadn't yet fathomed. It was exciting to imagine what kind of service God had in mind for her. She knew the principle of the talents in Luke 19:11–28 meant that though one may not have many talents, everyone had something. The key was not to bury yours in the ground!

Fired with enthusiasm, Joni looked around for ways to boost her self-image and to find gifts that God had given her.

Boosting her self-image meant first dealing with her appearance. She knew appearance didn't make one a better person, but when one took care of oneself, it would mean one was taking care of all that God had given. Joni enlisted the help of Jay and Diana in getting to look like her old self.

The girls experimented with makeup and hairstyles. They shopped for clothes that would be attractive and at the same time comfortable for sitting in a wheelchair.

The transformation had an immediate impact. She became more comfortable around others her age and felt much more confident.

Her renewed confidence helped her to deal with the fact that she still needed other people and that she needed them to do such basic things as dressing and undressing her, or emptying a plastic bag attached to her leg for collecting urine.

A further result of her renewed confidence was her increased focus on the needs of those helping her. She took great lengths to express appreciation for the many duties they performed for her. She admitted that there were times in the past when she had been selfish, and she was committed to not letting it happen again.

Joni's interest in art and music was renewed. She began drawing with her mouth as her therapist had taught her. She formed a singing group with Dick, Diana, and several other friends who sang so well together that they eventually performed for Youth for Christ functions. Joni's enthusiasm for such things was not discouraged by her parents. They were willing to put up with loud music late at night while they watched their daughter grow more confident and positive about life.

Joni's enthusiasm and desire for service led her to become involved as a counselor for a neighboring Young Life Club. She was still close in age to the girls in the club who were going through traumatic and difficult experiences as teenagers. She understood their concerns about personal appearance, popularity, and choice of career. Many of them did not come from families like hers that supported her, and so she reached out openly and with love, knowing that the girls needed someone who would understand them.

Remembering how restless and unsatisfied she felt as a teenager, Joni stressed the importance of God's Word in their lives. Only His Word could give hope and stability. To gain their trust in such a message, she shared her own weaknesses and failures.

Joni's relationship with the girls wasn't just focused on deep issues. She and her associates put on hilarious games and devised all sorts of parties to create a normal atmosphere for a teenager.

Her success as a counselor for Young Life gave her an opportunity to serve at a summer camp in the Rocky Mountains as a counselor. The change in scenery and the opportunity to serve was so exhilarating, she did not mind remaining a spectator during many of the activities. The girls felt bad but Joni encouraged them to go on without her.

"Don't worry about me! It's sweet of you to ask, but it's a real treat for me just to be here in such marvelous scenery."

Although Joni could not participate in many of the activities, her ministry was special when it came to Bible study time. They got over the initial shock of having someone in a wheelchair be their counselor and were able to focus on the task at hand—learning how to live for Christ and discovering how He had gifted them. The kids accepted God's message in large part because she identified with them so well.

The approach of fall brought more changes. Steve was headed for college and the thought of losing a teacher and a friend discouraged Joni. She wondered how she would fare without him.

"I'll pray for you, Steve, but I'm going to miss you badly."

"You'll be okay, Joni, I promise you. God won't let you down. You'll still have His Holy Spirit to guide and teach you. It isn't as though I'm walking out on you forever."

The two corresponded after his entrance to Columbia Bible College in South Carolina, and Joni's life continued on at a normal pace.

Despite the normalcy, a vacuum was beginning to form in Joni's life. Now twenty-one years old, many of her close friends were getting married. Though she was happy to serve as a bridesmaid at their weddings, it soon became apparent that relationships with such friends were changing. They now had other concerns, and so Joni's circle of friends slowly disappeared.

Seeing her friends marry, Joni wondered if she too would marry someday. She had not yet met anyone whom she felt comfortable with and that could fill her need. Giving up Dick would seem to have been unwise, given his love for Joni, but she was convinced that it had been the right thing to do. The question of who else God might have in mind still remained unanswered.

Joni prayed about a future partner but did not dwell on it. She accepted, too, the fact that she might be single the rest of her life. It was not an attractive thought, but one which she honestly expressed and committed to God.

Imagine her surprise a short while later when a young man came to visit one Saturday.

9

*D*on appeared to be just another guy interested in kids when Joni first met him at a Young Life leadership meeting. And when he asked her if he could come around to her house sometime for a longer talk, she did not think it unusual. She had lots of her friends—some guys, some girls—just come around to talk. She responded with a casual air.

"Why not. Just drop in anytime."

He did. Early the next morning!

"Wake up, Joni!" Jay's voice broke into her pleasant sleep. "You've got a visitor—name of Don."

"Tell him to hang on. I'll be there as soon as possible."

Because Joni's routine to get up in the morning took some time, she had plenty of opportunity to think over her impressions of Don the night before.

She had remembered that he was older—twenty-seven—and stood out in the crowd with his striking good looks. You couldn't forget him in a hurry!

He seemed to be of strong character with his own opinions but hadn't steamrolled people during the meeting. He took time to consider subjects under discussion.

When Don and Joni finally began talking that morning, she found that the two had a lot in common. Morning turned into lunch and she invited him to stay. Conversation continued and soon it was dinner time, which Don conveniently enjoyed with Joni and the family.

Joni was intrigued with Don's life and commitment. He described his work with inner-city kids. It wasn't just a stunt for him. He really cared, and it warmed Joni's heart to see someone so dedicated to such a needy cause. And he seemed to enjoy her company. A lot.

When asked if he could come back for a visit the following morning, Joni was flattered but couldn't grant his request.

"Sorry, Don, but tomorrow is my day for classes at college."

Don left reluctantly that evening and a little disappointed that he could not see her the next morning. No surprise, then, that he showed up on campus the next day as Joni came out of her last class. It seemed to Joni as if he was drawn to her as a magnet. Her reaction was a little guarded to such attention.

When Don showed up again the third day at her home, she felt he was being a bit presumptuous. But Don was an engaging man and she soon grew to like him.

Don was a valuable person at Young Life meetings. He showed a depth of knowledge of Bible truths but a pleasing sensitivity to the feelings and opinions of others. He never deviated from the truth, but he wasn't prepared to force his point of view with wordy arguments. People respected him for his uncompromising yet gentle stand.

Joni admired Don for his spiritual insight but at the same time couldn't fail to notice his strong physique and dark, handsome looks. It was flattering to be sought out by someone of his calibre. Since she had left the hospital, she had been content to be one in a crowd of friends. Now she was having a special relationship with someone like Don and her feelings for him grew.

It wasn't long before her feelings, and his, came out in the open. Beginning as a strong attraction toward each other without romantic attachments, the two grew to like each other more and more.

Joni told Don one of the things she liked so much about him.

"With most folks, my chair seems an obstacle, but it has never mattered with you. It's a welcome change."

The expressions of mutual liking grew into something much stronger over the next few months. Her lessons in a positive self-image were beginning to bear fruit. It felt good to be admired as a woman again.

As the weeks progressed, they discovered different facets of each other's life. Their initial attraction to each other had been because of their love for Christ and their willingness to serve Him in any service to which they were directed. They both felt their role was to nurture and encourage young people. That common bond drew them closer and closer to each other.

"We'd talk for hours, sharing God's Word and what each of us had learned through our individual Christian experiences," she wrote later of her relationship with Don.

Discussions about the Bible and young people were not the only ways Joni and Don spent their time. They had a lot of fun being together and enjoying leisure time.

On one summer day, Don took Joni down to the seashore. The scenery was refreshing. She gulped huge amounts of fresh salty air and enjoyed the sounds of gulls overhead. Hearing the breakers crash on shore brought back many memories.

Don had other ideas about their excursion. He hadn't brought her to admire the scenery from the parking lot. He grabbed the handles of the wheelchair and began dragging it across the sand. She was going to enjoy the ocean up close!

It was rough going at first, maneuvering the chair over the deep, soft sand. When they reached the shoreline where it was wet and compacted, Don picked up speed. He took the wheelchair up to the edge of the water, the last bit of each wave wrapping around the wheels.

"What on earth are you doing?!" Joni shouted, struggling to make her voice carry over the breeze and waves. She was half scared, half intoxicated by the novelty of the situation. Onlookers on the beach looked perplexed at this crazy drama in front of their eyes.

Don was not content to keep her in the chair, so close to the real experience. He scooped Joni out of her chair and carried her into the waves. Joni savored every moment of the experience—the feeling of power at her feet and of the strength of the man that held her in his arms.

Expeditions like those to the ocean brought the two closer together. As autumn arrived, Don chose other ways to spend their leisure time. He pushed her chair up steep mountain trails, picnicking at the top and enjoying the view.

Joni had always been honest with herself, and she questioned her deepening relationship with Don.

Where would it all end? she wondered.

The thought of ending the relationship as she had with Jason and Dick was painful.

Would it be necessary to undergo the self-torture for a third time? Was this friendship going to become just another casualty in my life?

Joni continued to call it just a friendship because she was afraid of letting her emotions run away with her.

Be careful, her head kept warning her heart. *Remember how you have suffered previously. You don't want to go through all that again.*

Yet the more time they spent together, the more difficult she found it to take her own advice. This was most often true when she accompanied Don during his work with his street kids. She liked what she saw, and she knew it was not an act to impress her. He cared deeply for the kids who had received a "raw deal" in life. They could give him nothing in return, and so she knew he was not on an ego trip. He was there to put them in touch with the living Christ. Joni, as well as others, could not help but respect him for that.

It was difficult to keep Don at arm's length. She respected him, enjoyed his company, and was attracted to him. His words and actions one day made the inner turmoil even more difficult. Leaning over her while she was sketching outside, Don spoke the words, "Joni, I love you."

Joni repeated the words to him, but the lightness in her voice signaled to Don that she didn't have the sense of commitment for which he was looking.

"Joni, this is something much more. Don't you realize, I'm falling in love with you." Don bent over to kiss her in order to underscore his meaning.

In any other circumstance, it would have meant a casual kiss of friendship to Joni. But Joni knew that for her, imprisoned as she was in her wheelchair, it meant something much more serious. It meant a new phase for their relationship.

She tried to ward Don off gently, without hurting his feelings. Joni knew he was genuine enough on the surface, but she wondered if he had thought the whole thing through. Being married to her would involve a lifelong commitment to a quadriplegic. Their marriage would be subject to stresses and strains that ordinary couples never faced. Although he had a strong personality, she doubted whether or not he would be able to handle such a delicate and demanding obligation. It would be enough to daunt most men.

She mulled over the incident in her mind after Don left that day. Not being able to sort out her feelings, she shared her struggle with Jay and Diana. She knew that she could depend on them for their honest opinions and their support. And both would be discreet.

"Be careful, Joni," urged Jay anxiously. "It's a tricky situation. I'd hate either of you to get hurt unnecessarily."

Diana's reaction was similar.

"Cool it, Joni. I'm glad for you that you've found such a good friend. But it might be better to keep it that way. He's obviously genuinely fond of you. It's easy to see that. For the time being, please be careful."

———————

Circumstances provided the time and the means necessary for Joni to "cool it" with Don. Jay offered Joni the opportunity of coming to live with her and her daughter. This provided Joni with several benefits. First, she would be able to live more on her own, just like other young women her age who had moved away from home into their own apartment.

Second, she sensed that though her parents loved having her, the strain her accident and subsequent rehabilitation caused was reason enough for her to move away. It would give them a needed change from the constant care they provided. Jay was staying at the family ranch, which meant they could still get to see Joni quite often.

Third, Joni could provide adult companionship to Jay and could also help by being with Kay if Jay ever needed to go out.

It was even more convenient for everyone because Diana had married and moved to a house near the ranch. And Joni's other sister Kathy was also close by. This meant

Joni's support circle could be nearby and share in the duties.

These all combined to make the move a wise one for Joni, and the family got to work making the necessary changes.

10

Moving into the ranch with Jay was no simple matter. It required a great deal of remodeling in order to make the house accessible. And a wing was added to accommodate Joni.

Joni's father did all the work himself. He built the room to let in as much light as possible with a large picture window. The window also gave Joni a beautiful view of the countryside. He also lined the walls with wood paneling and built a stone fireplace.

Joni remembered the room vividly in her book *A Step Further.* "[It was] a converted slaves quarters with ceiling beams my Dad had gotten from an old clipper ship . . . The walls were spotted with Dad's rugged paintings of scenes from the old West. The handwoven Indian blanket gave it the final touch of atmosphere to this cozy hideaway."

John Eareckson went about building the wing with the same intensity and dedication as he had used when he built a home for his wife years earlier. Though older and suffering with arthritis, he met the challenge and used all his skills to create a suitable and comfortable environment for his youngest daughter.

John's example provided a lesson for Joni. She remembered the way in which he rebuilt the barn that had burned down twice and how he had done it with cheerfulness in spite of both financial and personal loss. Watching him build her new room showed her again his resolution and determination. She witnessed these qualities and admired them even more now that he had to deal with greater physical limitations. His testimony taught her that she need not accept the worst and become a vegetable wasting away in a wheelchair while other people waited on her.

Both Joni and her father, despite their determination and energy, would be the first to admit that whatever they did or achieved was because of the power of prayer and their deep faith in the purposes of God. And their life was also filled with many mistakes, which sent them back to the drawing board. Life was not always clear sailing.

―――――――

Life at the moment, however, seemed ideal. Don shared Joni's enthusiasm for her new home with Jay. He continued his relationship with Joni, taking her on hikes, picnics, and other outings with greater frequency. He attended to Joni's needs as a quadriplegic without embarrassment. He also treated her as a normal, attractive young woman.

Joni felt safe with Don and yet she was still frightened about the future. *Where was all this leading?*

"I've learned to care for him a lot," Joni expressed to Diana one day. "I'm just worried that he couldn't cope with the next step. I love him too much to saddle him with a lifetime commitment to my difficulties." Diana was even less sure about the relationship. Diana even went so far as to share her concerns with Don directly.

"I appreciate your concern," he had replied. "But it's not necessary. We're old enough to know what we're doing. Granted, there would be problems, but I'd propose to Joni straight away if I thought she'd have me."

Each time the subject of their future came up, Joni shared her reservations. She did not want to be accused of manipulating or rushing Don into marriage. She would have to be totally honest with him, even if it would cost her a great deal of pain if he were to leave.

Don minimized the potential problems. "We could get a mobile home for a start and I could do the basic chores until we could afford outside help. My love for you is great enough to do without much of the physical side that a normal couple enjoy."

Joni was not sure that Don could do without the kind of physical love she thought he needed. Even though her doctors had told her that she could bear children, she knew that she couldn't express her love with the tenderness she longed to give him because she was deprived of feeling from the shoulders down.

Would it be enough?

She dreaded the thought of her husband not having enough physical love in addition to being tied down to her physical needs.

Joni's needs for a husband never became desperate. She knew her circumstances and accepted the inevitable. But that did not keep her from being attracted to other young men. There would be no lack of suitors in her life as evidenced quite humorously on one occasion.

A nice-looking young man had turned up on her doorstep. He had driven quite a long distance, asking to speak with Joni. Naturally, she made him feel welcome and began a friendly conversation.

The young man seemed rather uncomfortable while Joni continued her attempts at putting him at ease. Eventually he blurted out, "God has revealed to me that I should propose to you. I want you to become my wife."

Gently, so as not to hurt his feelings, Joni explained to

him that at least ten men over the last couple of years had come to her with the same message.

The young man was puzzled. He stressed his confidence that God had directed him to do this.

Joni did not give him his marching orders immediately but took the time to explain the concept of God's guidance as she understood it from the Bible.

"God wouldn't deliberately mislead any of His people," she stressed, "it's more a question of us misunderstanding Him."

––––––––

Joni felt secure that she had not misled Don and that she understood how God was leading. She was confident that the steps toward their marriage were right and that God had finally allowed her some happiness. Jay and Diana expressed reservations but Joni floated on cloud nine.

It was not until Christmas that a small cloud of doubt appeared on the horizon. They had a small argument which was quickly resolved. But the incident led to her becoming more possessive. She wanted to be with him all the time. She felt jealous when he talked with other girls.

Her feelings began to affect her Bible reading and prayer time. Don reacted strongly to the change in Joni. He resented her attempts to tie him down. He wanted a certain degree of freedom. Joni apologized for her possessiveness but still had reservations in the back of her mind.

Don decided that a literal separation would be healthy for their friendship, and so he set off for a tour of Europe with a friend for three weeks.

The separation was simple for Don but difficult for Joni. She had to remain at home, anchored to a wheelchair. She was at the mercy of the postman delivering postcards. Only Don's affectionate greeting upon his arrival reassured Joni that there had been nothing to worry about.

———————

Dealing with God's guidance was not limited to questions regarding her relationship with Don. The subject of healing came up several times in her talks with Don. *Perhaps this was the time?*

Thinking about the possibility opened old wounds. She remembered her bitter disappointment when she expected to wake up healed after an all-night prayer vigil at her family's church. Yet the next day there was absolutely no change in her physical condition. Now the potential of marriage made the desire for healing strong enough to put aside her remembrances of past disappointments.

Joni's desire to be healed was not only stronger, she felt, but she now understood that perhaps she did not have enough faith the first time around. The second time around would be different.

She and Don, after prayer and reading of Scripture, were certain that it was God's will that she be healed. Elders at the church laid hands on her and anointed her with oil.

"I began to pray for healing in Jesus' name. . . . In order to show genuine faith, I called my friends on the telephone and said, 'Hey, you, next time you see me I'm going to be standing on my feet.' I even went to a couple of 'faith healing' services. I was convinced that my healing was in God's plan . . . but nothing happened."

———————

Joni's disappointment at not being healed was compounded by her closest friend's continuing doubts about her relationship with Don. Diana expressed her doubts even though it was difficult to do. Joni would have preferred that Diana be overjoyed at the prospect. Joni saw Don's arrival on the scene as God's provision for her since Diana had recently gotten married. The timing seemed perfect for Joni.

Joni mistrusted Diana's motives at the time but came to value her friend's loyalty and love. She had, after all, put her career on hold while she spent time looking after Joni. That love would later receive a tribute from Joni in *A Step Further*.

"Diana did more than listen. She shared. Now sharing your deep thoughts, fears, and concerns with another person is a scary thing. It's making yourself vulnerable. But isn't that much of what love is all about?"

Diana continued to pray for Joni, standing in the wings in case she should be needed.

Don became withdrawn and introspective after the hoped-for miracle did not occur. He began spending more time in activities that did not include Joni.

When Steve Estes returned home from college, he and Diana got together to discuss why God did not answer her and Don's prayers for healing.

"I'm sure God wants everyone to be healed, Joni," Steve said. "You will be healed one day, but perhaps not until you receive your glorified body. It may be if you did receive sensational healing, the press might distort the whole situation. In that case, it wouldn't bring glory to God. It's even different in our modern culture in the States in contrast with more backward areas of the world where missionaries have seen healing miracles. God may be using that means for them to speak to their hearts because so far they may not have the Word of God written down in their own language."

Diana agreed with Steve. Both gave Joni much food for thought, but she did not discuss the matter with Don.

Though they still got together often, he still seemed somewhat introspective. Not only did they avoid the subject of healing, they also avoided the subject of marriage.

The subject could not be avoided for long, however, and the inevitable day arrived when it would come out in the open. Joni detected an element of tension in Don's voice.

"I'm off to New York this summer, counseling in a Young Life camp. I've got to leave tomorrow."

"How come 'goodbye'? I'll be seeing you again after a few weeks, won't I?" Joni was glad to hear that there would be another interlude in their relationship just like the one they had when he went to Europe. She thought they needed more time to sort out their attitudes and emotions. Don did not need time, however.

"I'm desperately sorry, Joni. The last thing I want to do is hurt you. We should never have allowed our friendship to develop so far. Marriage for us is out of the question. It was a mistake."

Joni could hardly believe what she was hearing.

"You can't just walk out of my life like that! It was you who encouraged me to think and hope of a shared future together. We've become so close—you can't mean you were just stringing me along."

"No, that wasn't my intention at all. But I've come to see it was wrong. I couldn't handle marriage with you and all the problems it involves."

Joni sat helplessly in her chair, sobbing with disappointment.

Don walked away from her.

"I'm sorry, Joni, but I mean it. I've given it a lot of thought and I know it's right."

Joni pleaded with him to reconsider and take the time for more discussion. Don was resolute.

"Goodbye, Joni," he said and shut the door behind him.

11

J oni's paralysis did not exempt her from feeling the pain of a broken heart. Self-pity as well as resentment consumed her thoughts. The change in Don's personality and love for her after all the tenderness that had passed between them was inexplicable. *God, what are you doing to me?* she cried.

She told herself that Don was being "cruel to be kind," and that an abrupt severing of their relationship was far better than a slow, lingering death. But Don's "kindness" would be easier for him to bear. He had an active life in which to throw himself and forget the past. Joni, by contrast, was limited in her ability to forget. She had to spend hours in her wheelchair without distractions.

Forgetting Don was not easy. She heard news about him from youngsters they'd both been trying to help. And memories of their time together—hiking, picnics, talking—flooded her heart.

It was painful for Joni to confess that she only had herself to blame. She should have heeded Diana's and Jay's advice. They had had no ulterior motive. They had only wanted to spare her the agony of rejection, but she had been blind to their warnings. She had managed to persuade herself that marriage to Don was part of God's perfect plan for her life.

The healing of Joni's heart would not be accomplished by sitting and waiting. It required, as did her physical rehabilitation, outside help. Diana and Jay stood by her as they had always done. Even Dick encouraged her.

"I was devastated all that time ago when you wrote to me saying that you just wanted to remain friends. It hurt badly but I've got to admit now that you were right. My feelings for you never changed, yet I came to realize I couldn't have coped with all the problems of marriage to someone as disabled as yourself."

Steve Estes provided his encouragement via letter when he heard what had happened.

"God knows what He's doing, Joni," he pointed out. "You'll be a better person when you've come through this trial. God always deals with us in love."

Encouragement from many people helped but ultimately it was Joni's relationship with her Lord that made the difference. Turning to 1 Corinthians 13, she realized that her love for Don had not reflected the love that God valued. Her love had become possessive and demanding.

God's Word also led her to be thankful, not only for the life she still had, but for the pain of losing Don as well. She would be grateful even in years to come for what she learned in the loss.

"My life changed more during the last half of 1972 than any other period of my life—even in my previous five years in a chair," she recorded concerning the experience.

Joni had always been too dependent on other people for her faith. Her human props had included Dick, Jay, Diana, Steve, and finally Don. She was grateful for their support but realized that it would be God alone upon whom she would rely as a "shield, strong tower, and the shadow of a great rock in a weary land."

God's strength enabled Joni to let go of Don in her heart

and face the future. Even when she heard of Don's engagement to a woman called Sandy, she did not go to pieces as friends had feared she might. When she finally met Sandy, she was able to congratulate her sincerely and without reservation.

"I'm so glad for you both. I pray for you every night."

With the important lesson of dependence upon God alone finally learned, Joni turned her attention to the future again. She was grateful for the opportunities to counsel other young people. She was frequently asked regarding her experience with Don, "How can you accept the fact that you will probably never marry? It must be shattering."

Joni's answer reflected the maturing she had experienced.

"Right now I don't know whether I will or not. But one thing I am sure about. God has some great things in store for me in a future day. No one, disabled or able-bodied, has the right to expect marriage automatically. And if God withholds something we may greatly desire, He will provide other compensations beyond a shadow of doubt.

"If you give back to God your right to marriage, He may well later on introduce someone else in your life. But clutching on tightly to people or possessions is fatal. You only end up feeling frustrated and full of anxiety."

Joni's relationship with the young people grew deeper. They felt that they could listen to Joni because it wasn't head knowledge that she shared from textbooks. Her knowledge was developed in the midst of traumatic experiences. In turn, Joni grew even more deeply as a result of her time with the young people. She saw again the benefit of her trials. Helping to solve their problems sharpened her skill to solve her own. And giving messages of hope and challenge helped her focus on what she might be doing with her time and talents that God had given her.

One talent that Joni knew needed more attention was her art. She enjoyed drawing illustrations from time to time, but she now tackled the challenge in earnest and with a fresh approach. Her positive outlook on life was reflected in the subjects she chose and the way in which she treated them.

People responded warmly to her art, but Joni was a stern taskmistress when it came to her work. It wasn't enough to be admired because of her unconventional and difficult method of holding a pen in her mouth. She wanted to be appreciated as a serious artist without people making allowances for her physical problems.

The more Joni drew, the more pleasure she derived from the results and the greater dexterity she acquired in using the tools of her trade. It became an important tool for her, just as Chris, her occupational therapist, had predicted it would become.

Joni's favorite tool was a felt-tip Flair pen. It provided the right texture and size for her mouth and teeth to get the proper grip as well as lay an even coat of ink on the paper. Years later it would become a trademark, and she would never travel without one in order to sign the many autographs people requested of her.

As her confidence in her work grew, Joni experimented with different sorts of paper and various pens, pencils, and even charcoal. Soon she was producing beautiful artwork for birthday, Christmas, and wedding presents for friends and family.

Joni enjoyed giving her artwork away, and the thought of someday selling her work regularly rarely crossed her mind. She did have the opportunity at local festivals to display her artwork but it was rarely a big commercial success. She usually gave it away.

But one afternoon would change all of that.

A businessman named Neil Miller called on Joni's father one day in his office. Neil was one of those men whom Joni later described as a Christian who "saw opportunities where other people saw obstacles." While he and Mr. Eareckson sat discussing business, Neil was impressed by a painting he saw on the wall. He verbalized his admiration, thinking it was done by a professional artist.

He was staggered to learn who did the painting and how it was done.

"Joni holds it with her mouth," the proud father told him.

"That's absolutely amazing! Fancy accomplishing all that and reaching such a high standard without training! Has she ever put on an exhibition?"

"Not really," replied Joni's father. "She gives most of it away."

Neil had other ideas. "Well, leave it with me. If you don't think she'd mind, I would like more people to appreciate her talent."

Joni did not have to wait very long.

Neil phoned back to say that he had arranged a modest exhibition at a small but exclusive restaurant in central Baltimore.

Joni worked hard, finishing off and selecting a suitable range of drawings. She had no idea what to expect. She thought that a few people would drop in casually to examine the work and that perhaps one or two of her pictures might be sold. She was grateful for what she thought was to be a modest, yet more publicized display of her work. It would give her a chance to see if her artwork was appreciated because of her art and not because of her disability.

Joni could not have anticipated the lengths to which Neil

would go in order to publicize the exhibition. On the way to the restaurant, Jay and Joni noticed that there was a large amount of traffic. They asked the policemen who directed them around the traffic what had happened.

He ignored the question and waved them on, too busy to handle inquiries when he had to manage traffic around a big brass band that was playing outside the restaurant! And across the front of the restaurant was a large banner reading, "Joni Eareckson Day." Television crews and a growing crowd of onlookers gave the impression that a politician or celebrity had arrived.

"Help, Jay. Let's get out of here!" Joni pleaded.

Despite her embarrassment, there was no way Joni could be excused from attending her exhibition. Jay was finally able to drive to the front where Neil assisted in transferring Joni out of the car. She was soon surrounded by television reporters and cameramen. A lovely bouquet of roses was presented to her, and the mayor declared "Art Appreciation Week" to be officially open.

Joni was the first featured artist!

12

"*D*id you have to organize an event on this scale?" she asked Neil. She had hoped for an honest appraisal of her artwork, yet all the attention to her disability, and not the exhibit, made her uncomfortable.

There was no time to honor Joni's objection. And she later learned that she need not have feared how her work would be accepted. Reporters fired questions at her which she quickly learned to enjoy answering. She saw that she had an opportunity to communicate that disabled people are real people and not second-class citizens. She made it a point that each person, even a disabled person, wants to be assessed on his or her own merits.

Neil Miller knew more about Joni's merits than Joni did. After several more questions about her choice of subjects and her technique and her lack of training, Neil was able to pull Joni aside and talk with her privately.

"You underrate yourself, Joni. You must learn to appraise your work for its true value. I must apologize for all the razzmatazz, but I guess I'm first and foremost a showman. I don't believe in a half-hearted affair."

Neil had more than showmanship in mind that day. He left Joni for a few moments and returned with a young man in tow. He left them together without explaining the purpose of his introduction.

Joni tried one or two conversational gambits without getting anywhere. She knew there must be a way to get through the exterior of his unhappy expression. She could only try more superficial questions to perhaps strike a clue.

"What sort of job do you have?"

"I used to be a fireman but I'm no longer able to work because of an accident." He stopped, biting his lips and holding back tears that welled up in his eyes. "Well . . . er . . . Mr. Miller told me you had a difficult time learning to live with your handicap," he said.

"I'll say I did! I was so depressed when I learned the full extent of my injuries, I badly wanted to commit suicide. Only there was no way I could take my life without the use of my hands. I even went so far as to beg my friend to do it for me."

Gaining confidence from Joni's honesty and interest in him, the young man pushed his arms toward her.

"Look, I've only been left with these stumps after a fire!"

Joni saw with horror the charred ends of his arms where his hands had once been. She could guess from his outburst how sad and hopeless he was feeling.

"There's no future for me. I'm finished," he added.

"Hang on there. I'm sure I can help you. Even more important I can point you to Someone who has stood by me through all my troubles."

Joni introduced her special Someone by first sharing her experience in the hospital and rehabilitation center.

"It's only natural that you are bitter and depressed at first. Most people would have exactly the same reaction. And it must be especially tough for a fellow who wants to earn his living and provide eventually for a wife and family. I do sympathize."

The noise of the crowd around them did not interrupt Joni's testimony.

"Without Him I could not possibly have faced up to all my fears and difficulties," she said.

She concluded with the story of her commitment to Christ many years ago at Young Life Camp. She did not press the young man to make the same decision she made. It seemed evident to her that he needed time, just as she had needed time, to wrestle with his feelings and the situation in which he found himself.

Joni was content to know that a seed had been sown and that the young man felt encouraged. The fact that God used her that day meant more to her than being the guest of honor at an exhibition. For half an hour, the young man had been her guest of honor, invited to be there by the sovereign hand of God.

When at last Joni brought herself back to the world of art and the event, she was astonished to learn that she had sold about a thousand dollars worth of pictures!

Joni was enthusiastic about her success. It was more than the money about which she was enthused. It meant that her art had value and that perhaps she could gain some financial independence as well.

The benefits of the exhibition did not stop there, however. Joni's artwork was shown on a major Baltimore station. Soon after, they invited her to take part in a local chat show to talk more about her paintings.

A columnist belonging to a Baltimore newspaper first asked the question that had begun to be on everyone's minds.

"Why do you put the letters PTL on all your drawings?"

Joni's response was left unaltered in the article the reporter wrote.

"It means Praise The Lord. You see, I know God cares for me—for everyone—so anything that happens to me He has planned for my good. Even in my wheelchair He has given me contentment."

Joni's reputation as an artist took off. Invitations flooded in. Even an able-bodied person would have tired from all the engagements Joni was asked to keep. Joni had to be considerate of not only her own limitations, but those of her helpers as well. She visited church groups, Christian women's clubs, schools, civic functions, and any other group who wanted to hear her testimony as well as see her paintings.

An invitation soon arrived from the White House to visit President Nixon and his wife, Pat. After a tour of the presidential home, Joni spent time with the First Couple and presented them with one of her drawings.

What a striking contrast the scene was! Five years earlier, Joni had hung suspended by a Stryker Frame over a linoleum floor, wondering if there was any value to life. Now she sat in the White House with the President!

There was no let-up in the flood of requests for interviews after that. And the more she became known through such interviews, the more her art sold. To meet the growing demand, Joni produced a series of greeting cards and also had prints made from a selection of drawings. A corporation was formed to handle production and marketing of the cards and prints. The company was called PTL.

The success of PTL led to the fulfillment not only of Joni's dream but also of many other Christians in the Western Baltimore area. Many people had prayed for the establishment of a Christian bookstore. They thought it would not only meet the needs of Christians in that area but also help people who had no connections with the church at all. Joni and two others joined in a partnership and made the dream a reality.

The bookstore was opened in September of 1973 as Logos Bookstore. It was located in a shopping mall. There was a lot of work involved in setting up the store—work in which Joni could not participate. But she was an active partner in every stage of planning and making of arrangements. She also sold her original artwork through the store.

The store and exhibitions of her art gave Joni the opportunity to share her testimony in writing. She printed her testimony, which was handed out at art shows by her helpers. It first described her artwork and then told of her relationship with Jesus Christ.

It was hard for Joni to imagine during those days why or how she could have contemplated suicide. In the introduction to *A Step Further,* Joni described it this way:

"It's hard to believe I ever had thoughts like that. In fact, I almost can't remember what feeling that way was like. . . . My artwork and my supportive family and friends helped to pull me out of my depression. But the heartfelt gratitude I have for this life in a wheelchair could only have come from God and His Word."

Just suppose she had succeeded in suicide, or less dramatic, had refused the therapy that enabled her to sit up in a wheelchair . . . or turned down the tuition from her friend, Christie Brown, to help develop her creative skills.

God's sovereignty in all things was becoming clearer each day. And each day Joni was able to articulate her feelings and the Word of God more effectively. Her many public-speaking engagements in the year that followed the opening of the store gave her the skills she would need— and need much sooner than she could imagine.

Joni received an exciting phone call one day.

"I'm speaking from the 'Today Show' in New York," the caller said. "How about appearing on our program to tell your story and show some of your drawings. Can you make it?"

Joni's heart skipped a beat. What a scary prospect! But

she rose to the challenge and accepted the invitation.

"Okay. I'll be pleased to come."

It would be a once-in-a-lifetime opportunity to spread her message across the country.

Joni, Jay, and two other helpers drove to New York a day before the interview in order to relax and get settled. The following morning she was taken to the recording studios to discuss the program with the director. A short while later, Joni found herself on the set with cameras and the famous Barbara Walters. She shot a quick prayer to heaven when the red lights of the cameras went on.

13

G od guided the interview beyond Joni's expectations. Barbara Walters posed her questions in such a way that Joni enjoyed answering them. She felt at liberty to share her faith as well as talk about her experiences.

Jay greeted Joni off stage after the interview.

"Quite possibly you have spoken to twenty or thirty million people this morning about your faith."

Statistics like that were a great encouragement to Joni. What a marvelous opportunity. It made the tiring journey and hassle worthwhile.

Among the millions of people who watched Joni that morning were the president and vice-president of the Papermate company that manufactured the Flair pen used by Joni on the show. When they noticed her using the pen, the company was quick to contact her. A promotional tour was arranged by Papermate so that Joni could exhibit her art.

National exposure brought with it a greater potential to lose perspective and "burn out." But Joni was able to avoid the many problems of national exposure by practicing key principles.

The first was her commitment to focus on individuals, even in the midst of large crowds or hectic schedules. After the Today Show interview, she spoke at length off stage with one of the other guests—the wife of a U.S. Senator—about her faith and values.

But it wasn't just famous people to whom Joni paid personal attention. Her love included those whom many would either ignore or push aside. One such instance took place in a bookstore at which she was signing books.

Joni was hurriedly autographing to help the long line of people move quickly. In the distance she could hear grunting and groaning. The noise got closer with each autograph she signed.

Finally Joni met the source of the noise face-to-face—a severely disabled girl who was unable to speak intelligibly. The shaking hands, twisted feet, and drooling mouth gave evidence that the girl had cerebral palsy. Not only was her cerebral palsy severe, she also was without the kind of helpers Joni had that would make her appearance very desirable. In fact, the girl was dirty and unkempt.

Joni was not put off by the girl's outward appearance, however. Long association with disabled people had helped her to discard feelings of revulsion and prejudice that many people experience when they meet a severely disabled person. She had learned to dig down and find what the person was like on the inside.

The girl's name was Nadine and the "digging" proved worthwhile. Joni spent an hour with Nadine after the book-signing and learned a lot about her. She was the same age as Joni and was very intelligent. They spoke about their faith in Jesus, and Nadine shared some of her poetry with Joni. Her poetry revealed that Nadine had come to terms with her disability and did not blame God. As Joni described her impressions of Nadine, she felt that Nadine "knew what it meant to experience the joy of the Lord, the peace that passes all understanding."

Joni's attention to individuals and their feelings did not always come naturally. One incidence in particular taught Joni the importance of responding to what people said and felt.

A twelve-year-old girl named Kathy, best friend of Joni's niece Kay, was visiting with the family one day as she had done quite often. Jay and Joni invited Kathy to watch a Billy Graham crusade that was being shown on TV that evening. Kathy had always been a lovable extrovert, and so when the show concluded she blurted out, "Well, if I were right there in that arena, I would have gone forward."

Jay and Joni had not intended to put Kathy under any pressure, but when Kathy shared her feelings, they knew it was time to counsel Kathy. Joni, being the closest to Kathy, was expected to be the one to lead Kathy to Christ. Unfortunately, Joni did not respond immediately. And then one event led to another in the coming days and Kathy's interest was pushed on the back burner.

It was Jay who confronted Joni on the matter.

"Have you spoken to Kathy yet?"

Feeling guilty for neglecting what was obviously her responsibility, Joni snapped at Jay.

"No, I haven't spoken to Kathy. I haven't had time yet!"

"Well, how come you have no time for your niece's best friend even though you've time to travel all over the country?" asked Jay wryly, free to speak her mind as Joni's sister.

Jay's question hit Joni hard. Lying in bed later that night, Joni's tears flowed down on the pillow as she acknowledged to God that she had missed several chances to have a serious chat with Kathy. Having asked for His forgiveness for the unnecessary delay, Joni drifted off to sleep.

Early the next morning Kathy came by to visit. Obedient to God this time, Joni led Kathy to the Lord.

"It was obvious that the Holy Spirit had already done His work as the 'advance man,' softening her heart and opening her mind," Joni wrote later of the event. It not only brought a new believer into the kingdom, it also molded Joni's heart to be more responsive to people.

Joni's attention to individuals benefitted not only the person receiving the attention, it was also a blessing to Joni. Rick Spaulding was an excellent example of how Joni learned so much from people she met in her travels. Joni met him in Philadelphia where she was speaking. She remembered that he wrote letters of encouragement to her quite often.

Rick, twenty-three years of age and brain injured, became disabled when he fell and hit his head on the gym floor.

"The most he can do is to turn his head and blink his eyes," his mother explained to Joni. "It took him months to learn even that tiny movement."

Joni visited with Rick at length and learned that his disability had not kept him from getting good grades in college. He communicated by blinking toward a letter chart until his mother could understand what words he was trying to spell out. He would dictate essays and test papers this way, also. He studied texts by listening to them on tape.

Joni conversed with Rick, mostly by asking "yes" or "no" questions. She enthused with him over one of her favorite topics—what it would be like in heaven when they got their new glorious bodies.

"Think of it Rick . . . we'll be on our feet—running, walking, working, talking with Jesus—all kinds of things!"

Rick joined in the excitement by rapidly moving his eyelids.

Her attention to heaven was a second key principle that

guided Joni during her worldwide ministry. She knew where she was going and that other people could someday join her in heaven with her Lord. She made every attempt to communicate the reality of heaven, especially to other disabled people.

Joni's longing for heaven was nurtured by many people, including Corrie ten Boom. Tante Corrie had suffered terrible depravation in Ravensbruck concentration camp. She had also lost her dear sister Betsie and her beloved father at the hands of the Nazis. Their only crime had been to conceal Jews in their attic when they were in danger of being carted off to death camps. Corrie and her family sheltered as many as possible until they were discovered, knowing full well what the punishment would be.

After the war, Corrie traveled widely, taking God's message of love and forgiveness to needy people. She also wrote about her experiences in her books, which led to a meeting with Joni.

Joni and Corrie were both at a publishers convention one day. Seeing Joni in her wheelchair, Tante Corrie rushed forward to greet Joni, ignoring the crowds that had gathered around both of them. She grasped Joni's slim fingers with her own work-worn hands and greeted her.

"One day, my friend, we will be dancing together in heaven because of the Lord Jesus," Corrie told Joni.

The thought of heaven was an exhilarating prospect for Joni. She devoted the last chapter of her book *A Step Further* to discussing what heaven meant to her and what it would be like.

"Suffering does more than make us want to go to heaven. It prepares us to meet God when we get there." That's what Joni wanted most of all—to meet God. She did not want to go to heaven because she was disenchanted with earth or her physical condition. To illustrate her motives for desiring heaven, she described what it was like to return home in the days when she was still on her feet. Her mother would welcome her in the kitchen and her father would be anxious to hear all about her day.

"For Christians, heaven will be like that," she wrote.

A third guiding principle for Joni was the importance of maintaining an honest and optimistic perspective on one's disability as well as one's potential. It meant pursuing every opportunity to grow and to try things while at the same time realizing limitations.

Joni had not always viewed life in such a way. Her love for art was not always as intense.

"I remember when I had a 'ho-hum' attitude toward art," she confessed in her book *Seeking God*. It was an art teacher who made her examine great masters and discuss techniques, color, and composition. Joni's boredom turned to joy as a result.

"The more I looked at works of art . . . the more I understood, the more I felt joy."

Having to pursue opportunities and experiences did not come naturally on every occasion. Years after her love for art had been rekindled, Joni was forced to spend a long time lying in bed in order for a pressure sore to heal. The experience of lying on the bed without a chance to get up was a depressing one. It was her newly found friend Ken who encouraged her.

"God's compassions never cease or fail," Ken reminded her. "They are new every morning."

Putting muscle to God's Word, Ken set out a way to make the time pass quickly for Joni and to keep her artistic skills sharp. One day he brought her heavy art easel into her bedroom. Joni was puzzled at his actions.

"I can't use that while I'm lying on my back. It's tricky enough when I'm sitting in my chair."

"Wait and see," promised Ken. "We can spread the tripod right over your bed. . . . With a few pillows propped here and there, you'll be able to reach your canvas."

A lesson in optimism learned.

Lessons in realism also had to be learned, as well as communicated. Her talents led her to meet so many people, including those who had not received the same gifts or blessings she had. Some were more disabled, others were less.

Joni acknowledged in *A Step Further* that "there are always those below us (on the scale of suffering) who suffer less, and those above who suffer more. The problem is we usually like to compare ourselves only with those who suffer less. That way we can pity ourselves and pretend we're at the top of the scale."

Joni was realistic and honest about her place on the scale at various points in life.

"This is the way it has been through the journey of my life so far, hills and valleys, a few steps forward, and the odd one or two back. All sufferers are prone to self-pity at times, self-aggrandizement, and complaining. It is only through God's grace that we can triumph at all."

It was not always easy to encourage people to take a realistic view of life and to be honest with one's situation. Too often, people looked for a way to fix a problem quickly, or in some cases lead a friend or relative to Christ instantly.

A year or two after writing her first book, Joni still received many letters that tugged at her heartstrings. The letters often described someone in the family who had become paralyzed through an accident. Very often the writer of the letter would ask Joni to send an autographed copy of the book to the accident victim in hopes that her message would help the person recover.

"I'm sorry, but I won't," was often Joni's reply. She

admitted that her heart went out to such people. But she had reservations about giving the person a book. She realized from her own history that it would take a long time for the person to accept their disability. Advice from a total stranger would not help anyone who was not seeking advice. It was better, she felt, to give the person time and space to want to seek out help. Help would always be there and the message would have greater impact, Joni felt.

———

Grounded in her relationship with God as well as strong guiding principles for being in the public eye, Joni continued to receive many invitations to speak all around the country. Her engagements ranged from art exhibitions to speeches to TV and radio. Her calendar was so full it was impossible to imagine that commitments could be kept. But God would stretch her and train her through this schedule for a ministry that lay in the years ahead. Every appointment kept today would mean a lesson learned for tomorrow.

14

*B*y 1975, Joni had become a nationally known celebrity. She was much sought after by convention organizers and the media. Her testimony and her artwork continued to capture everyone's attention and imagination.

Looking out over the crowd of two thousand young people at a Youth for Christ rally in Kansas City one evening, Joni thought back over the previous eight years and the many people who had had an impact on her life. Under the lights, seeing all those young people, Joni could objectively say that her growth in grace during those difficult teen years had been made possible by people who took the time to invest their lives in her. She could not pat herself on the back. God had used people to impact her life in a marvelous way.

And now it was her turn to do the same for these and other young people. It was gratifying to find that after she shared her testimony with young people like those in Kansas City, the kids were committing themselves to Christ in increasingly large numbers.

"Being able to impact even one person would make the past eight years in the wheelchair worth it all," Joni remarked about her impact on young people.

The impact on audiences everywhere was in large part

based upon Joni's gift of being able to identify with the audience. She had credibility with them because it was readily apparent that she had suffered.

They also identified with her honesty. Someone had tried to encourage Joni shortly after her accident by saying, "Remember all the crowns you'll be given in heaven as a compensation for your suffering."

"I'd much rather be back on my feet," was her tart reply.

That honest portrayal of herself was always balanced with an exhortation. Eight years later she could encourage the audience with these words: "I'm really happy. I wouldn't change my life—I even feel privileged."

Joni made it clear to everyone she met that her life was still in process. She did not consider herself to have "arrived" by any means. Her life was much like that of "Christian" in John Bunyan's book *Pilgrim's Progress.*

Joni had certainly met similar characters and circumstances as the main character in the allegory. She had met friends like Diana, whom she could call Faithful. And there was her friend Steve, who played the role of Evangelist. She had been imprisoned in Doubting Castle for a while and had been bogged down in the Slough of Despond. She had even escaped the clutches of Giant Despair.

Unlike *Pilgrim's Progress,* Joni's journey had not yet been completed. The path ahead was uncharted and filled with potential dangers, but she was gaining confidence that God would be with her the farther she traveled.

Encouraged by the increasing impact that her message was having on people, Joni agreed to write a book about her life. Teaming up with Joe Musser, Joni began the laborious process of dictating the many details of her life into a concise account of how God had worked. As difficult as the process would be, it was a book that needed to be written.

"What happened on July 30, 1967 was the beginning of an incredible adventure that I feel compelled to share because of what I have learned."

Joni's purpose in writing the book was highlighted by the apostle Paul's words in 2 Corinthians 4:8: "We are handicapped on all sides, but we are never frustrated; we are puzzled, but never in despair. We are persecuted, but we never have to stand alone: we may be knocked down but we are never knocked out!" (Phillips translation).

Joni readily agreed that her sufferings did not match Paul's, but she could not help but identify with him when he wrote, "I've been spat on. I've been beaten . . . I've spent time in jail. I've been shipwrecked. And to crown everything . . . He gave me . . . a thorn in the flesh to keep me from becoming conceited."

Joni did not likewise demand her readers to keep a stiff upper lip at all costs and deny the difficult circumstances or their emotions. "There is a time to laugh . . . and a time to mourn," she reminded them (Ecclesiastes 3:4).

The book helped people realize that they needed to rise above their trials through God's strength, just as Joni had done. God would never give any of His people a burden that was too heavy for them to bear. He measured each person's capacity for suffering and allowed it accordingly.

———

No one could have imagined how successful Joni's first book would become. The book was breaking new ground. The subject of disability had not been aired in that way before. In fact, most people tended to sweep such topics under the carpet. Disabled people were often isolated from the community instead of being integrated into it. Children with mental or physical problems were usually kept apart in special schools, whereas today, wherever possible, they are accepted into ordinary neighborhood schools. Joni's book, in addition to providing spiritual guidance and encouragement, taught people a different view of those with disabilities.

Making people aware of the issues regarding disability was not without its dangers. Joni had to speak frankly and freely about every aspect of her quadriplegia with little embarrassment. In her book *Choices . . . Changes,* Joni shared, "My books *Joni* and *A Step Further* were a risky uncovering of my life. . . . Why do I put these things in a book? Obviously, I hope to play a small part in building up your faith in Christ."

The first book kept being reprinted to meet the demand. It was translated into other languages and distributed around the world. Its impact was as deep in the hearts of people as it was wide.

"I was surprised and pleased to receive thousands of letters from people who could identify with my bouts of depression, despair, and loneliness," Joni wrote later. The kinds of subjects raised in those letters did not deal strictly with disability. Lonely single people, parents, people experiencing a nervous breakdown, young people struggling with temptations, and those contemplating suicide all shared with Joni how they were feeling and how her life had ministered to them.

Joni did not entertain the thought of writing a second book, but the response to her first book and the need to address some of the issues raised in the letters compelled her to do so.

Because Steve Estes had been such an encouragement to her in the past, and because of his depth of knowledge of the Bible, Joni asked him to join her in the project. He was married and attending Westminster Theological Seminary at the time.

Steve and Joni spent a great deal of time working on *A Step Further*. The book was published in 1978 and became a bestseller. It met a deep-seated need for many people to explore God's perspective on all kinds of issues related to suffering and the sovereignty of God. It also included Joni's favorite subject—heaven.

———

Prior to the release of *A Step Further*, Joni was approached by World Wide Films to take part in an exciting venture. They wanted to make a film of her life story. She discussed the matter at length with producer Bill Brown and Dr. Billy Graham as well as her family and friends.

She was warned by everyone, including Dr. Graham, that the process would not be easy. Reliving old experiences and re-creating former relationships would stir up hurtful emotions. Joni knew the potential for being hurt but felt the impact of the film would far outweigh the few months of pain she would endure.

Joni moved to Los Angeles for the filming. World Wide made every effort to make her feel comfortable and secure. They rented an apartment for her near the studios. Jay and Judy Butler, Joni's new assistant on loan from the Billy Graham staff, settled into the apartment. Prayer support was also provided throughout the six months of filming.

Joni would need the prayer support. Just mustering the courage to participate was reason enough. She felt like a country bumpkin from rural Maryland in the sophisticated atmosphere of Hollywood. And she also took the courageous step of playing the part of herself in the film, wanting it to look as authentic as possible. Although stand-ins were used in parts of the diving scene, Joni acted out all of the parts, including the scene in which she floated in the water. The film crew responded to Joni's courage with consideration and encouraging words.

No expense was spared to turn out a thoroughly professional film. The best actors and technicians were recruited to ensure that Joni's story and the gospel would be communicated.

Joni found the experience of being a film star anything but glamorous. She had to endure the indignity of being strapped to a Stryker Frame again with a shapeless hospital gown and blond wig. It would not have been so bad if the scene in the hospital bed could have been shot just once. Many retakes were necessary to get the film just right. The scene in which Dick smuggled a puppy into the room required fifteen takes and four different puppies!

The strain was recognizable after a while. It was difficult to project herself back in time to those nightmarish first weeks in the hospital.

Relaxing with Judy and Jay at the end of the day helped to relieve the tension. Hollywood was a strange environment for all of them. Routines like shopping and eating out helped to restore normality in between shootings. Leisure hours also provided a refreshing change.

Jim Collier, the director of the film, had also been responsible for the film *The Hiding Place*, the story about Corrie ten Boom.

"She's praying for this movie," Jim told Joni regarding Corrie. Joni wondered if Corrie had handled the remaking of her life into film better than she.

Painful memories were renewed for Joni when the shooting of the film was moved to Ranchos Los Amigos

Hospital. Rather than feeling relaxed at the sight of the pens and brushes in the Occupational Therapy room, Joni found the emotions of self-doubt and anxiety returning. She was supposed to act the part of a nervous patient, handling the task of carving lines in soft clay. She didn't need to act. She really was nervous.

Joni joined the other patients at the hospital after the shooting was over. She made friends with many of them, not seeming to be a star by anyone's imagination. She apologized to them for her film making such an interruption in their schedule.

The interruption to the schedules of the patients at Ranchos Los Amigos could be forgiven. The impact that the film would have on the lives of disabled people there and in other parts of the world would make the interruption a blessing.

15

Joni seemed to live in two worlds during the making of the film. The world of movie-making was exciting and new. The people were interesting, and at times she felt just like anyone else without a disability. At other times, however, her disability spoke loudly and clearly, disrupting life's routines and joys.

———

Producing the movie had its humorous moments. In one scene, Joni was required to reenact the times when she and her friend Dick would get into the elevator and stop between floors. It was their way of ensuring privacy from other patients and staff while they talked and kissed. Jay teased Joni as she read portions of the script in advance.

"What do you know? In next week's script they've written in a kissing scene. How about that?"

Joni tried to appear nonchalant but it was not easy. Not only did she have to kiss a stranger, she had to do so while crammed into an elevator with lights, script lady, and camera crew.

The experience was not as terrible as she thought it would be. The experience of kissing was not all that unpleasant. *And it was just acting, after all,* she reminded herself. The scene was over in just a few retakes.

Acting in a kissing scene was not the only glamorous adventure Joni had. Unscripted relationships also occupied her time. One of the crew specialists headed the lighting team. He was known as the "gaffer" and took a special liking to Joni. He went out of his way to be kind and considerate to Joni, shading her from the intense glare of the lights and helping with her wheelchair when she found obstacles in the way.

"You don't seem handicapped to me," he remarked one day.

The compliment was not lost on Joni. She had always done her best to feel confident about herself and had hoped people would overlook her disability and get to know her as a real person. The gaffer's attention to her and his observation made a big impression.

The two enjoyed being together often on the set and off. On one occasion, they enjoyed dinner with Joni's sister Jay and her new friend Rob Tregenza.

Rob was a researcher for the film. Although there were many young men working on the set, Joni noticed that he paid particular attention to Jay. That was not all bad. Jay had been a single mom for many years and needed a friend. Rob provided a sympathetic ear. And from all that Joni observed about his personality and faith, she sensed that she would see a lot more of him during the coming months.

The dinner with Rob, Jay, and the gaffer was a delightful experience for Joni. The gaffer was quietly attentive throughout the meal and took special care to stride alongside Joni while Jay and Rob walked hand in hand behind them.

Joni could not deny that she enjoyed her friendship with a man who was not put off by her disability. So often she felt her disability got in the way of her relationships. She wanted to be treated as an ordinary person.

It was no surprise, then, that Joni accepted his invitation to go out on a date to a nearby restaurant. The date was everything Joni had wanted it to be. Her only anxiety was wondering whether or not her wheelchair would scrape the leather inside his gleaming red Porsche.

Joni felt special. She knew that she did not look disabled to any observer driving beside them on the highway. Her wheelchair was hidden away, and she appeared to be just like any other blond woman being driven by a man in a Porsche!

The date with the gaffer was special. She felt like a woman and very much at ease in the environment of the fancy restaurant. Her efforts to draw attention away from her disability included ordering something simple from the menu that she could eat with her specially angled spoon.

The world of film making, however, was built on illusion, and Joni had to face reality. Things and people were not what they seemed to be. This truth was even seen in the way scenes were filmed. Because filming had to be done in as short a time as possible, the autumn season had to be manufactured by the crew. They spray-painted the green leaves of summer's trees with red and gold so as to give the impression of fall.

People were also not as they appeared or did not take interest in things Joni thought were important. A lanky young actor called Richard was introduced to Joni as the fellow who was going to play Steve Estes in the film. As the makeup artist worked on the two of them, Joni began telling Richard how Steve had been able to help her with Bible studies. Richard interrupted her gently.

"Sorry, Joni, but I need you to fill me in on Steve's gestures and mannerisms."

Joni herself could not hide from the reality of who she

was and the disability with which she lived. As much as she enjoyed feeling like any other woman while on the date with the gaffer, she paid the price after returning home.

It was in the middle of the night when Jay heard Joni's frantic call.

"Jay, I've a pounding headache. My bed is soaking. I think my catheter must be blocked."

Jay worked fast and furiously to insert a new one while Joni's heartbeat raced. She felt racked with pain, and Jay's action did not make things better. The doctors had warned them that an emergency like this could happen at any minute.

"Quick!" Jay told the paramedics over the phone. They arrived within minutes.

Joni cried out to be relieved from her agony, "Praise the Lord . . . praise the Lord."

It would not be until 2:30 in the morning that Joni finally felt relief and was able to return to her room with the others. Her body was spared but she paid the price for it the next day on the set.

The routines of daily living also reminded Joni that normal life was an illusion. Just getting ready for the date with the gaffer had been a major event, given the choice of hairstyle, clothing, and makeup. It was not just that one date but throughout her entire life that Joni would have to remember her disability in choice of clothing or in going through the daily routines of getting ready.

Choice of clothing was not a simple task. She had to choose clothes that not only looked right and did not accentuate her disability, she also had to choose clothes that were practical.

"It's difficult finding clothes that fit well when you're always having to reach and pull and push . . ." she confesses.

Makeup and hairstyling presented other difficulties. With five different people being involved in her morning routine, what she looked like varied from day to day.

"On Monday, my hairstyle is an original creation by Irene. On Tuesday it has the Judy touch to it. . . . On Friday I come to work with a Lynda look," Joni described in *Secret Strength*.

No matter the style of clothing or makeup, the reality of Joni's disability did not disappear. That fact was brought home to Joni not only in her own life during that time, but also as she watched the other disabled that lived at the hospital where they were shooting the film.

Joni saw disabled people who had no family or friends to help them. They had been abandoned and left to rehabilitate on their own. They spent time with sullen faces, watching the film crew do their work. The image left an impression on Joni.

A disabled girl with polio named Debbie Stone was able to fill in the details on several of the patients' lives.

"Do you know, Joni, they've got both practical and spiritual struggles going on in their minds."

Joni wondered if there could not be some kind of outside agency that could step in and help. *Couldn't someone step in to be their friend?* Joni wondered.

Joni made special friendships during the time of the filming. The art director, Jim Sewell, was one such friend. The friendship and partnership would last for many years.

On days when Joni was not filming, Jim coached her on her artwork. Joni had several paintings to complete for studio scenes in the movie. Joni admired him greatly.

"James is a fine gentleman who has studied extensively and traveled all over the world," she recorded in *Secret*

Strength. "More than just an artist, he's a concert pianist, an accomplished writer, and a mathematician."

Joni felt privileged to develop a friendship with Jim. Although a meticulous taskmaster, he was always sensitive to her needs. Putting his arm around her shoulders with a warm hug, he would suggest a break in Joni's action and push her out onto the cool patio outside the studio.

The hills of Santa Barbara provided a welcome change of scenery in the filming for Joni. The hills were used to re-create some of the scenes of Maryland, and being there brought back memories of her time before her accident when she enjoyed nature so much. She had always been a country girl with her family.

Joni's love of nature was not lost, however, just because she was in a wheelchair. Her writings continually refer to God's creation. "Our God is a wonderful God," she once wrote. "Just one good look at . . . the beauty of nature . . . can tell us that."

Various anecdotes in her books also reveal the intense pleasure she felt from contact with nature. Something as small and as delicate as a butterfly would remind her. Sitting outside in her wheelchair one day, Joni felt a butterfly gently stroke her cheek as it flew around her. She felt as if it were a gentle stroke from God, encouraging her during a difficult period of her life.

The beauty of sweeping scenery also struck Joni. She climbed onto a chair lift on one occasion and went to the top of a high mountain that overlooked the wildlife reserve of Jasper Provincial Park in Alberta, Canada. "I marveled at the sight of a soaring eagle . . . a tiny speck against the distant mountain range. I watched as he circled . . . admiring his grace and ease."

On the same expedition in Canada, Joni was able to enjoy God's creation in a most unusual way. The rest of the family had taken a hike into the woods and left Joni behind at the campsite. She felt a little cheated at not being able to enjoy what they would see. She talked to the Lord about it.

"Lord, as I can't go off like the others to view your creation, bring me a special bit of it close to me so I can see it and really appreciate it."

Joni's prayer was not answered until a little while later after the rest of the family had returned. As Joni sat around the campfire, a small black bear approached Joni. He sniffed the cuffs of her trousers. She hardly dared to breathe, realizing her predicament.

The bear scampered off without incident but not before Joni was able to observe him in close detail. The other campers were not very happy at the thought of a bear intruding their campsite, but Joni realized it was a special answer from God for her desire to see His creation up close. She thought God must have had a sense of humor to have answered in such a way.

———————

Joni's life during the filming was not only a contrast between illusion and reality, it was also filled with many pressures and temptations. So much was going on all the time and so great an effort was demanded of Joni that she frequently suffered from exhaustion at the end of a busy day. She often found it hard to concentrate while reading. She had to read over a sentence two or three times in order to make any sense of it. Joni also became increasingly critical of herself and made little allowance for errors.

Joni's relationship with her Lord also suffered during that time. Prayer was never entirely forgotten, but it had to be squeezed in a much smaller space. She all but neglected her time of Bible study. She was feeling stale and jaded, a bit out of touch with her Heavenly Father. Only the guiding hand of God sustained her—a hand which knew that even the illusions and reality of disability she experienced while filming would someday be used for His glory.

16

God's vision for the film was not hidden from Joni. Despite the hectic schedule and the distractions from an intimate walk with Him, Joni kept His commands and His desire before her. Exhausted, tense, and weighing much less than she had when she left Maryland, Joni took advantage of every opportunity to follow her Lord.

Following Him meant listening to her old friend Steve, this time portrayed by an actor.

"All who become Christ's will have the same kind of body as His," Steve had told her. Though repeated by an actor, the words had the same impact. She clung to the thought that one day she would have a glorious body, perfect in every detail.

The image of herself with a perfect body in the presence of Christ prompted Joni to think of other people's eternal relationship with God. She prayed between scenes for members of the crew. She wanted every one of them to find Christ. She also prayed that when her film was released, it might influence people to recognize the claim that Christ had on their lives.

With the filming in California mostly completed, Joni

and the crew flew to Maryland for settings that could not be found in and around Los Angeles. It gave Joni the opportunity to be reunited with her family and for the crew to see where she had grown up.

The family reunion and the filming served as a fitting backdrop for Jay's marriage to Rob Tregenza. Their wedding was conducted in the living room of the farmhouse right after the last Maryland scene had been shot. The event was unpretentious and marked by genuine warmth and simplicity.

Joni was glad for Rob and Jay. She didn't envy them and was all too happy to see Jay find someone after the difficult life she had experienced.

Jay's marriage marked a turning point in Joni's life, and she knew things would never be the same. Although Jay had reassured her that their life together on the farm would still continue, she was not so naive as to think that things would be as they had been.

She did not let her thoughts or emotions show. She felt like an actor, not only in the film but also while off the set. No one could guess what she was really like behind her disguise. At times she even wondered herself.

Flying back to Los Angeles for a few more shots, Joni could sense things were not the same. Many of the actors had already left for work elsewhere. The weather was cold and damp. It was a complete contrast to the sunshine she had left behind.

The warm reception she received back on the set did not seem to lighten the burden. People could tell that she was tired. They were genuinely sympathetic and did their best to encourage her, especially since they heard of the recurring problem she was having with a pressure sore.

The makeup man encouraged Joni to make a speech to everyone assembled on the set. It was not easy for Joni.

"I want you to know how much I've enjoyed working with you . . . with help from all the team I'm sure many people will learn about the Lord. Those are my hopes for you also."

Joni's tears could not be contained. A close bond had been established between them. She was going to miss them, and she wasn't sure if her testimony to them had been a good one.

Her tears were interrupted by an announcement on the set.

"Billy Graham is here for a board meeting and would like to come over for a few minutes."

Joni's emotions of sadness were replaced by nervousness. Dr. Graham shook hands with everyone on the set as he approached Joni. When he finally reached her, he turned and spoke to the group. His point was simple and brief.

"People without Christ are far more crippled than Joni. The movie you have been working on will be a great encouragement to very many people with hosts of different problems."

Dr. Graham went on to thank them for their dedication and cooperation. He singled out Joni in particular.

"It must have been difficult for you, Joni, to recall those painful memories, but it will bring spiritual blessing to thousands of people all over the world."

Joni didn't feel she deserved the attention but was encouraged that Dr. Graham felt that way. Her sincere desire had always been to direct people's attention from herself and point them to Christ. *I don't deserve Dr. Graham's congratulations,* she mused.

Drifts of snow greeted Joni upon her flight back to Maryland where she would prepare to settle in with Rob and Jay at the ranch. Apart from a few wedding presents scattered around, she found things pretty much as before in her quarters.

Though the setting was the same, Joni sensed something was different. She was conscious of a strange feeling she could not explain. She realized it was she that had changed. Somehow, she did not fit anymore.

Such thoughts did not keep her from making the attempt at settling back in. Filming had left little time for her favorite hobbies, and so she returned to the canvas.

She stared at the blank, creamy surface. This was her first love. The subject had fascinated her from early childhood, long before her accident.

"Sitting on my dad's knee," Joni later wrote, "watching him swirl oils on his canvas . . . those are my earliest memories of painting. It wasn't long before I had my crayons out . . . from crayons I graduated to water colors, from water colors to oils."

Despite her love for painting, the magic would not return. Joni was out of practice, feeling frustrated. Nothing seemed to go right. Finally, with a scream of near hysteria, she knocked her supplies away in every direction with one sweep of the arm. Jay came running, alarmed at the noise.

"I can't draw! I can't do anything!" was all Joni could wail.

Jay attempted to console and encourage Joni, but it would be months before she would regain her confidence and ability. And there remained one last piece of the film that had to be shot before then.

The film required scenes of Joni's message at a Billy Graham rally containing thirty thousand people in Tampa, Florida. It would be the next to the last scene and serve as the climax to the message of hope.

As important as the scene was to the film, Joni felt like a hypocrite. She did not feel like there was any hope at the moment. She had meant it once but now she was not sure. It would take God's strength to get her through the scene.

The scene went fine as everyone had expected. God's working in her life was not to be preempted by her temporary setback. She fluffed the last few lines and choked with emotion at the conclusion. *I'm a total failure,* she thought.

———

Joni's recovery from self-doubt took several forms. God's truth would sink back into her consciousness slowly. A short trip to Los Angeles to re-record some garbled lines in the film diverted her attention. A visit to Grace Community Church during that time lifted her spirits slightly. Caring friends kept in touch, sending her get-well cards. Joni herself found comfort and encouragement from her friend Steve Estes on the pages of her well-worn copy of *A Step Further.*

When she at last came out of the depression, Joni found that it had been for a purpose. She realized that she could not sit in the comfort of the ranch and stagnate. There was more work for her to do and more challenges that God was preparing her for. Her decision to follow Him in the new adventure came before there was any clear direction. *Where would I go and what would I do?*

His marching orders surprised everyone, including Joni, when she announced that she was packing her bags for Southern California. It was time to branch out. Joni was thirty years old at the time, had written two books, and just completed a movie. It was time, she felt, to move into a more practical ministry.

I can't go weak at the knees with every fresh trial that comes my way, she told herself. *God needs mature, reliable Christians.*

The move to California meant leaving people she loved and who loved her. But she believed the decision was the right one. One practical reason had to do with the weather. The warm climate in California would be much more beneficial to her health. Maryland could get extremely cold in the winter.

The weather was not the motivator. It merely facilitated the mission to which she was called, that of somehow making life better for disabled people. She left Maryland with happy memories and excitement about the future.

I've been more than fortunate. I've always been surrounded by a caring family and lots of loyal friends. But it's not the same for thousands of handicapped people with no one to help them practically. Some even are without the comfort of God's Word. I'm sure this is what God is calling me to do.

Joni's move to California was wise, strategically speaking, given the mission she was about to launch. She was familiar with the staff at the rehabilitation hospital. Grace Community Church was sympathetic to her mission. And she had many contacts and friends from her association with World Wide Pictures.

Her parents were also reassured that Joni would not be alone. As hard as it was for them to say goodbye, they realized that at least Kerbe, Joni's cousin, would be living nearby and Judy Butler would be loaned to Joni for a year to get her ministry started.

———

Joni's arrival in California was accompanied by a little bit of doubt, but she realized it would simply take time to get used to the heavy traffic and the pollution. Such things would be a small price to pay for the success of the mission.

She was welcomed warmly and with practical help by many people. Furniture was installed in her new house. Visitors brought potted plants, ready-made meals, and many offers to help.

Joni also met an invaluable man named Dr. Sam Britten. He was introduced by Joni's pastor, Dr. John MacArthur.

"You really ought to meet him. He's involved with our outreach to the handicapped at church and is also director of a big unit at the university," Dr. MacArthur advised Joni.

Joni lost no time in finding Dr. Britten. His work involved himself in the lives of dozens of disabled people at one time at the university. He helped in the design of rehabilitation programs for disabled people. Joni was impressed by his work and was excited to share her vision with him. She was surprised, however, at one of his questions.

"Have you thought about driving a vehicle?" he asked.

"Well, do you think someone as handicapped as I would be safe to drive along the freeways?" Joni asked back.

Dr. Britten answered her question with a series of tests and exercises. He concluded that it would be possible, and though Joni was not convinced, she nevertheless was eager to find out if it might actually be possible. Her desire for independence outweighed her fear of Los Angeles traffic.

Joni's dream began to take shape in the coming weeks. Soon the ministry of "Joni and Friends" was born. Their first leaflet identified the mission.

"The purpose of 'Joni and Friends' . . . is to accelerate Christian ministry in the disability community. That means we call and equip Christians to do what Jesus commanded—to care for the weak and hurting people in our midst."

Out of Joni's confusion and depression, God had begun a new work in the image of His Son. All that remained was hard work and the help of many people.

17

*J*oni's ministry caught the attention of people immediately. Volunteers turned up with typewriting and
shorthand skills to deal with the many letters that
had come following the release of two books and a movie.

Joni's mission to accelerate disability ministry included
a variety of disabilities. "Our ministry is an outreach to
those with disabilities, such as cerebral palsy, mental re-
tardation, spinal cord injuries, muscular dystrophy, or mul-
tiple sclerosis."

No one at that time could have foreseen how the ministry would expand over the years. Joni's vision would also
be enlarged because by 1987 there would be 35 million
people with disabilities in the United States alone. And the
population was growing. Those with Joni's type of disability, for example, were increasing in number by eight thousand per year in the U.S. Worldwide, the numbers of disabled people were staggering—519 million by 1992.

Although Joni's vision was large and saw the needs of
all these people, she did not live her ministry only in
dreams. She practiced it day to day with real people.

Joni was intrigued by a woman named Vicky Olivas who
also came to Dr. Britten's center and was, like Joni, in a

wheelchair. She was not very friendly and stayed aloof from Joni's advances for friendship. Joni had heard that Vicky was seeing a psychologist, a hypnotist, and a spiritist all at the same time. *She must be desperate!* Joni thought.

It wasn't until Joni was going through therapy with Dr. Britten's assistant, Rana, that Joni learned the whole story about Vicky's life.

Vicky had been deserted by her husband and forced to go out job hunting to support herself and her young son Arturo. She went to an interview, feeling suspicious of the run-down area in which the business operated. She was even more suspicious when she met the boss. Her instincts warned her that all was not well, but it was too late to get away.

The business owner began to handle her roughly. Vicky resisted but the man reached for his gun and shot her. She slumped to the floor in a pool of blood.

"I didn't mean to shoot you . . . I really didn't!" the man protested.

"Please get my car," Vicky begged. "My keys are in my purse."

Vicky felt dizzy and weak. The room spun round and she called for help. A young girl rushed in and grabbed a dirty towel to stop the flow of blood.

"Take me to a hospital, please," Vicky pleaded. "Just say that you two were walking past and saw me lying shot in my car. I swear I won't get you into trouble. I'll back up your story."

"Okay," said the man. "We'll do it, but if you let on afterwards . . . I'll kill your son."

Vicky's plan worked. They left her at the hospital, telling the doctors the story that Vicky had concocted, and then fled. Once safe at the hospital, however, Vicky told the true story and the two were later arrested.

Joni was stunned to hear Rana tell Vicky's story. She was further taken aback when Rana said bitterly, "I don't know how you can believe in a God who would allow all that stuff."

What could I tell her? wondered Joni. *She's not ready for the whole truth, but I can't let this chance go by.*

Joni spoke her thoughts aloud.

"Maybe we've got to trust Him even when nothing seems fair. It's possible to have faith, to doubt, and still believe."

Joni hoped to somehow minister to Vicky, but it was Rana who would first come to Christ.

Joni's words regarding faith in response to Rana did not fall on deaf, or insensitive, ears. Rana's life was also a difficult one. Her reason for working at the hospital was to earn a diploma to teach physical education to handicapped high school children. There was nothing unusual in that, but the details of her private life revealed that she was ready for a change.

Rana was divorced and lonely. She had a twelve-year-old daughter and they were very close, but life did not make sense to her. Rana's anger toward God was natural. Joni finally found an opportunity with Rana to explain further.

"The reason why things like that (Vicky's accident) happen is sin. And that affects each one of us."

Joni sensed that Rana wanted to unburden herself but she was hardly prepared for what followed.

"I guess I know all about that," Rana volunteered. Then she spelled out the pattern of her life since her divorce. Rejected and bitter, she had deliberately set out to have a good time to try to compensate. One affair after another brought no satisfaction. She spared Joni no details of her sordid story. Would Joni be too disgusted to have anything more to do with her?

"None of us is perfect," countered Joni. "We're all capable of that kind of behavior. But the big deal is that God is ready to forgive us."

A few days later Joni was able to tell Rana specifically how Christ had died on the cross just to save her from those sins.

"I'll give you a Bible with marked passages for you to sort out yourself," Joni promised. "You'll learn far more by reading God's Word than hearing my explanations."

Joni's wisdom paid off. She was delighted the next day when Rana walked into her room with a spring in her step and a smile on her face that had not been there before. She hardly needed to tell Joni that she had trusted Christ as her Savior. Joni was thrilled for her friend's newfound happiness and freedom.

Joni wanted to see the same happiness and freedom in Vicky's life, but her ministry to her was not to be quite the same. Vicky was a very private person and harbored much anger.

Vicky was capable of even less movement than Joni. She was not doing well financially and had to care for her five-year-old son Arturo. She was at the mercy of whatever attendant was working for her at the time. They came and went with alarming frequency.

With a view toward winning her friendship, Joni invited her to dinner at a restaurant one evening along with Rana, Judy Butler, and cousin Kerbe. Vicky relaxed sufficiently to talk about her son Arturo. Sensing how she loved Arturo and how she longed for encouragement, Joni ventured to bring the name of God into the conversation, suggesting that He could have the answer to many of Vicky's problems. Vicky stopped talking after that, however, and was fairly quiet the rest of the evening.

Rana confronted Joni after they dropped Vicky off.

"Look, Joni, we can't offer all the answers to Vicky on a plate. We have to earn the right to give her advice. Her setup is quite different from yours."

Joni felt hurt that a young Christian like Rana would be more sensitive, but upon reflection, she acknowledged that Rana had a point. Writing later in a book, Joni described an important lesson she learned.

"Jesus has made a difference in your life. You're convinced He will do the same for your disabled friend. The truth is, we cannot make someone a Christian. . . . Forget imposing your faith on your disabled friend. To expose your faith is so much easier . . . and so much more natural."

Joni should have known what Vicky's response would be. She herself had responded the same way in the hospital after her accident. She looked for other ways of reaching Vicky.

Dr. Britten provided some insight for Joni in this regard. One day while he was working with a disabled person near Joni, he commented, "I went over to see Tante Corrie this past weekend."

Joni's ears pricked up. Any news of Corrie ten Boom was always welcome. Joni had a deep love and respect for the woman who was now confined to bed after a stroke had left her unable to speak and move. Corrie was still very much aware of what was going on around her, and her charisma was still apparent in spite of her poor physical condition.

"I'm so glad I was able to alleviate her problems a little," Dr. Britten continued. "It was only a question of setting up a pulley system so she can exercise her weak arms. And I taught her attendants how to lift her in and out of bed with the least discomfort to her."

Joni listened as the words she needed to hear in her ministry to Vicky were spoken next.

"Now, after ninety years of hectic life, she can only wait in silence and pray. But the strange thing is I felt I had received a blessing just by being in her company."

Dr. Britten went off to help someone else but his words remained with Joni. She would attempt to reach Vicky in another way without appearing patronizing or forceful. She found an opportunity to let Vicky try on one of her surgical corsets which supported the back and enabled one to talk and even sing more clearly. The gesture opened a door of friendship.

Vicky spent the afternoon with Joni and the others that day. Joni described more of the details of the treatment she received in hopes that Vicky could pick up some pointers. She also tried to interest Vicky in trying some artwork.

The investment of time paid off in a small, but shocking, dividend. Vicky finally opened up and divulged that one of her attendants had tried to smother her with a pillow.

"Fortunately, my brother was in the house and heard me scream. Arturo and I can't go on any longer like this. We need help—badly."

Neither Joni nor the others could provide the help Vicky needed. It would be quite some time before Vicky received help or made the choice to follow Christ. In the meantime it seemed ironic that Vicky's life was so horrifying while Joni's life was filled with so many blessings.

Joni divided her time between the office and the physical therapy recommended by Dr. Britten. The therapy was designed to condition her muscles for driving a van. She did the exercises mostly to improve overall fitness and never imagined that she would someday be able to drive. Dr Britten, however, had other ideas.

Joni approached him one day and entered into a conversation while he was polishing a van in the parking lot.

Their conversation continued for a bit until he turned to her.

"We recognize your very real needs at the start of your new ministry," he explained. "So our elders put the facts before the church and their contributions have bought this for you." He pointed to the very van he was polishing.

Joni was speechless. She was overwhelmed by the generosity but was unsure that she would be able to use it. She had, after all, only been practicing her muscles and didn't have the opportunity to actually drive.

Dr. Britten was undaunted and confident. He showed her where the mechanical lift would be placed and how her wheelchair would fit. "Just some more work for you in the gym and some work on this van and you'll be ready."

Various adaptations and mechanical adjustments had to be made but at last the great day arrived. Once into the van and locked into position, Joni started the ignition with a push of her mouthstick. She then inched out onto the back streets, still a little unsure of herself.

The next hurdle was the driving test. She was told to wait a week to take the test with other disabled people, but she was insistent in her right to take the test like everyone else. She won her right and used a pencil attached to her wrist. The test was followed by an exam on the open road with an examiner. He was fascinated with Joni's driving techniques, and though her equipment and methods were unusual, he had to admit that she fulfilled all of the requirements.

Joni passed!

"Yippee! At last! For the first time in fifteen years I can actually go out by myself. If only my folks could see me now."

She didn't wait long for that wish to be answered. Mom and Dad Eareckson traveled out just to see their daughter drive and offer congratulations. Their ride with Joni as driver was tense at first, but they eventually loosened their grip on the seats as they realized Joni was in full control.

Another step of faith on their part came as Joni announced she was moving to a new house farther out of the city. It required making a financial commitment, and being parents, they worried that she was taking on something beyond her ability to control. It was a natural thought for parents of a handicapped daughter, but they realized she was an adult and her determination and strength were equal to the task. Seeing the support she received from Grace Community Church also made the process of endorsing her move an easier one.

Joni moved to her new house while the Earecksons were with her. They jumped into the move wholeheartedly with helping to furnish the house and shopping for essential equipment, including dog toys for Joni's Scruffy!

Joni reflected on the blessings she had received from the Lord—blessings of family, finances, friends, a purpose in life, and most important of all, a relationship with the God who created her.

But what of Vicky? And what of people like her without hope and in some cases in danger? Though Joni would wait for God to touch someone's heart, she did not wait to act on the burden He had laid on her heart.

18

Joni sat with Rana and Judy and described what she had observed about Vicky's life and about her own.

"There's no program I know of to educate helpers to carry out these necessary tasks," she said despairingly.

Rana broke in, "Well, then, why don't you train other people to do the sort of things we do for you?"

"Yeah, that's a brilliant idea! Why haven't we thought of that before?"

That roundtable discussion led to the first "People Plus" conference in 1980. More than a hundred people crowded into Sam's lab, some in wheelchairs, some on respirators. Many parents, teachers, and nurses joined the meeting. Speakers spoke on various subjects regarding how people can accept and help disabled people. One of the speakers from Grace Community Church spoke on the subject about how even mentally disabled people can have an understanding of the love of God.

God used "People Plus" as an instrument in Vicky's conversion. She began to be less aggressive and less secretive. She was more open to discussions about spiritual truths. Joni still did not pressure Vicky but encouraged the openness.

As much as positive events like "People Plus" and encouraging words helped Vicky, it was experiences of adversity that brought Vicky to the Lord.

The first adversity belonged to Joni. She had been speaking and traveling quite often in those early days and had very little rest. It took a toll on her body.

"I'm afraid you'll have to stay in bed for a couple of months," warned the doctor. "That old pressure sore of yours has burst open again."

Joni had to "put the brakes" on her traveling and lie out in bed. Some people might have thought that Joni had suffered sufficiently when she broke her back in 1967. Wasn't it reasonable to suppose that no other misfortunes would befall her?

"Not at all," commented Joni. "Life will not flow smoothly for me automatically." She was still prone to the ordinary mishaps and disappointments that cropped up from time to time, but felt increasingly that God would give her the grace to endure them. Routine days without major problems were sometimes difficult to get through for her.

"Some days I can handle only so much . . . my weak shoulder muscles ache from holding up my heavy head . . . my back gets tired from sitting in one position . . . my neck gets a crick in it from looking up at everybody standing around me . . . God only gives me grace for today."

Trials had come to Joni on a regular basis, wrapped in frustration. Once, having just been released from the hospital, she met with a nasty accident. Her friend Sherry was pushing her wheelchair across a parking lot where they had been attending a youth rally. They hit some black ice, sending Joni out of the wheelchair and onto the frozen surface. Joni's immediate inward reaction was to cry, *Haven't I suffered enough already? Why did this have to happen?*

If it wasn't her body breaking down, it was her van.

"I just can't get used to trials," she wrote in *Secret*

Strength. "Like the other day when my van had a flat tire. My first thought was, 'God, you've got the wrong person for this one. Remember? This is Joni—the one who's paralyzed. I can't exactly hop out, flip open the trunk, grab the jack, and spin on a spare.' "

Joni's first reaction, therefore, to learn that her pressure sore was open again was seasoned with much experience in the Lord. "Okay, they happen to everyone . . . but James has some sage advice for people like me. 'Consider it all joy . . . when you encounter various trials, knowing that the testing of your faith produces endurance' " (James 1:2–3).

Telling herself the truth of God's Word was not quite the same as living it. Proclaiming a philosophy of stoicism is easy when things are going well. But Joni's spirits were at low ebb during the enforced bed rest for the pressure sore. She suffered a good deal of physical discomfort and fretted at the delay to her ministry.

Joni was bemoaning her condition when Rana wheeled Vicky into Joni's bedroom. Joni apologized for her attitude, but Vicky would have nothing to do with her apology.

"It helps me to see you real, struggling like the rest of us."

Watching Joni in her condition, weak and forlorn, gave Vicky the courage to confess how often she had envied Joni and resented the way people praised her attitude toward life.

"I thought—she hasn't got half the problems that I have to cope with. Why do folks make such a fuss over her?" she said to Joni.

"I know just how you feel," Joni broke in. "I often think that way about paraplegics who can use their hands and not rely so much on other people."

So although Joni did not relish her forced stay in bed,

she was at least thankful that it deepened her relationship with Vicky. After that frank exchange of what they saw in each other, they would always be honest. It was an important step in the right direction.

The second trial that brought Vicky to Christ came after Joni recovered from the bout with the pressure sore. As soon as it was healed, Judy and Rana accompanied Joni and Vicky on a holiday trip to a Bible camp in Estes Park, Colorado.

On the second night of their journey to the camp, the phone in the motel room rang. It was Vicky's mother. She called to tell Vicky the bad news that the Mexican currency had become almost worthless overnight.

It was disastrous news to Vicky who had all of her investments in Mexican currency. She had been living off of the interest on those investments.

Everyone was stunned. It seemed Vicky could not handle another crisis in her life. They all feared for their friend. Could it be the last straw for her?

"Want to go back to Los Angeles?" Rana asked.

"No—guess we won't achieve anything that way. Let's go on."

Their Bible reading that evening was all the more poignant because of Vicky's circumstance. It came from Psalm 60:15. Vicky herself read the verse out loud:

" 'Call upon me in the day of trouble and I will deliver you . . . and you will honor me.'

"Sure, this is a day of trouble," remarked Vicky wearily. "I know I'm weak . . . and it makes sense that I'll only get stronger if I put my faith in Christ. Don't you agree?" Vicky asked the others.

Vicky eventually answered the question herself, just as Rana said she needed to. Her time at camp and the months with Joni and Rana had brought her closer each day to that point.

Not only did Vicky surrender her life to Christ, she also served Him with what she had been given. She joined the team of "Joni and Friends" in order to counsel severely disabled people. Her personal experience proved invaluable to those who were going through traumatic experiences just as she had.

———————

While Joni was seeing disabled people come to Christ as a result of her ministry, she also said goodbye to a close friend. Corrie ten Boom had become severely disabled herself when she suffered another stroke.

Joni went to visit Tante Corrie. They could not converse because Corrie had lost all ability to communicate. She had to use gestures and the expressions of her face to convey her thoughts. Joni's and Corrie's favorite topic, heaven, brought the greatest response and joy from Corrie.

Joni described her longings for heaven and concluded by singing a song to Corrie.

Though I spend my mortal lifetime in this chair,
I refuse to waste it living in despair . . .
He has given me a gift beyond compare.
For heaven is nearer to me,
And at times it is all I can see.

Corrie tapped the rhythm on the arm of her chair. After the song, she prayed, although only the Lord could interpret her garbled speech.

As they parted after tea, Joni had a sense that the next time they met they would be in heaven.

———————

Joni's life at this point was characterized by much fruitfulness. Her walk with the Lord was growing daily, the ministry was growing, people around her like Vicky and Rana were responding to the gospel, and volunteers continued to help with all aspects of her life—ministry and personal.

But to Joni it seemed she was no nearer to a close relationship with someone special, which she had always desired. She was over thirty and thought every once in a while about the hopes she had as a teenager of being married someday.

God knew Joni's heart and carried out His plans in a rather humorous way.

Joni found herself in church one morning listening to a guest speaker who did not capture any of her interest. She tried as best she could but he continued to drone on.

Out of frustration, Joni decided to spend time in prayer for the remainder of the service. In order to be focused in her prayer, she decided she would pray for someone in particular. In this case it was a man who sat two or three rows in front of her. She did not know him or anything about him. She did not know what his face looked like. She only saw the back of his head.

Joni prayed for the man's health, his spiritual growth, any struggles he might be experiencing. She became so carried away in sincere prayer, she was surprised when the service came to an end. She knew that even though she might not have learned much that morning, she at least had prayed thoroughly for one individual.

Months passed and Joni nearly forgot the incident. After a morning service, a friend introduced Joni to a rather oriental-looking man. *Could it be?* Joni wondered. She asked him to turn his back to her. Seeing that it was the same person for whom she had prayed, she explained her interest in the back of his head and what she had done several months earlier. They both laughed and parted company, but not before Joni learned that his name was Ken Tada.

Ken and Joni bumped into each other quite often at various church functions. She got suspicious that her friends were trying to set her up with Ken when they were both invited to the same birthday party. Her suspicions were mixed with pleasure in that she was in no way averse to getting to know him better. She felt relaxed and comfortable in his company and liked his slightly shy personality.

Ken and Joni talked at greater length while at the party. Joni learned that Ken was a social studies teacher at a nearby high school, coached football, and was a third-generation Japanese.

"How about carrying on with our talk over dinner next Friday night, Joni?" he asked as they left the party.

"Sure, I'm free then. Thanks, Ken," Joni accepted.

Ken followed up on his invitation with a bouquet of yellow roses the next day.

Despite the obvious message Ken sent, Joni did not want to make too much of their first date together. First dates were often awkward with Joni's disability, and it had been a long time since Joni had gone out with someone.

Joni need not have been anxious. After instructions from Judy and Kerbe on how to lift Joni and handle the wheelchair, Ken proved to be most enjoyable company and very adept at making Joni feel at ease. She appreciated his humor and the way he anticipated her needs. He cut her food and held her glass of water as if he had been doing it a long time. She was also glad that her notoriety and her wheelchair did not put him off.

"I don't need to be afraid just because you're different," Ken remarked. That attitude helped their friendship blossom.

Times together became more frequent after their first date. Joni accompanied him to the sports club, admired his easy camaraderie with other fellows, and his grace and precision when he was playing on the racquetball courts. Being with him felt more and more comfortable.

Ken and Joni took a pause in their relationship as Joni headed back with Judy and Kerbe to Maryland for the Christmas holidays.

It was a very special Christmas. Jay and Rob had given birth to a new girl, Earecka, during the past year, and so Joni enjoyed holding the baby on her lap. And the familiar pattern of celebrations and the long-established family customs and rituals held Joni in their spell.

But not completely. God's ministry for her and thoughts of Ken had traveled back to Maryland with her and home would never be the same.

19

A nd Joni's life was not the only one changing by that Christmas of 1982.

Joni's parents, especially Johnny, were growing noticeably older. Though her father still had the "Cap'n John" spirit, his hearing and arthritis were getting worse. He still had a fondness for working with wood but he could no longer construct things. He settled for carving lamps, small tables, and stools. He still loved the outdoors and accompanied the family on outings, but he had to confine himself indoors during the wintry weather.

Joni received a call from Ken the last night she was in Maryland.

"Joni," her mother called her. "Here's a call for you. It's your friend from Los Angeles."

"Ken, is that you?!" Joni enthused over the phone. The two of them spent quite some time talking about what they had done while separated.

"I'll be back tomorrow, Ken . . . Yes, I do miss you."

Joni and the others packed all their Christmas presents the next morning along with their bags. Everyone shared emotional farewells. Joni also endured the teasing from her mom regarding Ken's phone call. It was obvious to her that he was special, although Joni wasn't quite sure just how special.

The following months would prove to her how much he

meant. They saw more of each other. Sometimes they drove out into the country or by the ocean. They acted like kids at times, riding roller coasters at Disneyland.

They talked often about their work. Joni outlined her plans for "Joni and Friends," and Ken told her more about his love for the kids in the Young Life Club that met on Wednesday nights.

Ken eventually shared with her how he became a Christian. And then he broached the subject of their relationship.

"I don't know why God brought us together . . . but I do know that I like being with you."

"Me too, Ken," replied Joni.

"I'm afraid, Joni. It's difficult when people our age start dating. It either ends up with them marrying or breaking up the relationship. I value our friendship. I don't want to lose it."

Though they were mature and desirous of keeping their friendship, the relationship was tenuous. After one particularly stressful evening for Ken, Joni surprised both of them by saying, "Our friendship doesn't seem to be getting anywhere . . . I think perhaps we should end it."

God did not let Joni think on that observation for too long. Her persistent enemy, the pressure sore, cropped up again. This time it looked particularly severe, and it appeared Joni would be laid up for a long time. Joni's brain whirled at the thought of all the cancellations and rearrangements that would need to be made as a result.

"Judy, call all my friends . . . anyone you can think of. I'm going to need prayer badly. And, oh yes, call Ken too."

Joni felt awkward when Ken arrived the next day with flowers and a gift. But Ken's relaxed demeanor and caring for her put her at ease.

Ken soon slipped into his old routine, reading to her and making meals on a tray for her to eat in bed. He also painted and decorated her house and did as much as he could to help her be more active, even though she was laid up in bed. The weeks passed by slowly, but Ken's patience and friendship made the waiting more pleasant.

The pressure sore healed after two months of bed rest. In order to celebrate, Joni invited her parents for a visit. Joni persuaded them to join Ken, Rana, Judy, and Vicky on a camping expedition.

It was a happy time for everyone. Joni revelled in being able to enjoy God's creation.

"God, you are so good to me," she said as she looked at the countryside and soaked in the sun that she had not seen for so long.

Ken and Joni used the opportunity while floating on the lake in a boat to express that they loved each other. Though Joni was sincere in her words, she wasn't ready for a complete commitment. Too many questions had not been resolved.

Some of the questions were practical ones. *What about housekeeping? What about kids? Could I have time for the ministry of "Joni and Friends"?*

Other questions were more emotional. She did not give away her affections lightly. There had been hurts and disappointments in the past. And she realized their relationship could never be as carefree as other people's.

There was also the feelings of both families to consider. Ken's family would face factors that they would find difficult to accept. There was the issue of her nationality. Ken was Japanese. She was a Westerner. Though Ken was born and raised as an American, his family was still very close to their Japanese heritage.

The problem of Joni's disability could not be ignored

either. It would make life much more complicated and expensive for Ken. Were it not for Joni's sincere and warm personality, his parents would not have been won over. Ken assured Joni that this was the case.

"Don't worry, Joni," he told her. "I'm absolutely sure."

Obtaining a blessing from Ken's folks was just the first step. Getting permission from Joni's parents loomed as a potentially larger problem. Ken was convinced that though he and Joni were older, and not required to obtain permission, things ought to be done correctly. Ken planned to bring up the subject over a game of Scrabble when the four got together.

Planning is one thing. Doing is another. Mrs. Eareckson seemed intent on playing the game rather competitively, and so Ken's attempts at bringing up the subject were delayed.

Once the game was over, however, the issue was discussed thoroughly. Much as they liked Ken and were glad for Joni's obvious happiness, they had misgivings. How would Ken manage financially? What about the very delicate situation of physical relationships with a quadriplegic?

Ken assured them that they had already discussed these matters honestly and were not viewing their love through rose-colored glasses. He answered their objections directly and yet with an open spirit. It was when he described his feelings regarding the matter of physical relationship that they became convinced that Ken, and the impending marriage, was a good choice.

"I know you've got our good at heart," Ken said. "It won't be easy—we shall have to work hard at giving pleasure to each other. Some well-meaning folks have even suggested that we go away together for a weekend, just to see how compatible we are and how I can handle it. Just a sort of trial run. But we couldn't. That would be falling short of God's standards."

The discussion with Joni's parents was not only good for Mr. and Mrs. Eareckson, it was also good for Joni. Listening to Ken made her realize just how deeply she loved Ken. His qualities as a future husband shone even brighter.

That is not to say that life before the wedding day was without tarnish. A few disagreements came, here and there, and blew over just as quickly. Joni was no saint, a fact to which she has alluded quite often.

"I'm only fallible and human," she said. "I may write books and speak at conferences and counsel people, but I'm just as prone to sin as the next person. It is by God's grace and God's power that I win through."

Her humble and sensitive spirit was also evidenced at her bridal shower. She had once dreaded the thought of how conspicuous she would feel, inadequate to unwrap her own gifts in front of other people.

"But I can honestly say I feel surrounded by love," she told her assembled friends. "And I'm so grateful that I'll be able to borrow your hands to use my kitchen tools, pots and pans, and my steam iron!"

A busy schedule of painting assignments helped Joni control the butterflies that were building as the day approached. And social engagements also occupied her time.

One special visit was with Ken's family as they celebrated his grandfather's birthday. Joni had already learned to love the entire family, but this was grandpa's eighty-eighth birthday and so she paid special attention to him.

She learned that he enjoyed hobbies such as writing poetry and painting, just like her dad did. She was eager for them to be able to meet, even though they could not communicate with each other. She knew that their common interests would cross the language barrier.

Joni also learned about her future father-in-law's painful

internment in a camp during World War II. She spent time with Ken's mom talking about cooking and discussed fashion with Ken's sister, Carol. She revelled in the opportunity to get to know all about them. Their culture was so diverse, but she did not allow that to be a barrier. Quite the opposite. She was confident that her family could learn so much from Ken's family.

———————

The great day, July 3, 1982, finally arrived. There had been a few tricky issues to deal with, such as a difficult-fitting dress, but things went according to plan. There were also no nagging doubts in Joni's mind. She felt at peace.

I'm glad we waited until we were absolutely sure, she thought.

The wedding itself was peaceful and full of joy. Joni had driven herself in the van with Judy to the church, her gown hanging in the back of the van. The bridesmaids helped her to dress, fastening the dainty heart-shaped necklace that Ken had given her around her neck.

Family and friends filled the sanctuary. Little Earecka waited eagerly in the wings to carry out her role as flower girl. Steve Estes waited at the front where he would assist the pastor in the ceremony.

Joni wheeled down the aisle behind her bridesmaids as the music played. Her father accompanied her, holding on to a cane with one hand and her wheelchair with the other.

Ken caught Joni's eyes as she got closer. His expectancy and love spoke to her heart through his eyes, and her whole being was filled with joy. The rest of the day flew by in a haze of happiness.

Joni and Ken boarded a plane the next morning with Judy and Rana for a flight to Hawaii where they would spend their honeymoon. Judy and Rana accompanied the couple in order to teach Ken how to bathe and dress Joni. The two helpers sat several rows behind the love birds on the plane and booked into a hotel several blocks from where Ken and Joni stayed.

Though Ken and Joni looked forward to privacy while on their honeymoon, Joni's notoriety followed her even to the beach on the first day. While Ken went swimming, a family noticed Joni on the beach and approached in excited whispers. Seeing them take out their cameras, Joni called out to them.

"I'm on my honeymoon. I'd rather not have any publicity."

"Fancy that!" the mother said, seemingly impressed with herself that she had such a wonderful story to tell her friends on the mainland. "And is that Mr. Eareckson?" she added as Ken came back to the scene.

Joni and Ken would hear that quite often from that day on. Joni would have done anything to avoid it, but both knew that the misunderstanding would never go away. Ken needed to be treated as a person in his own right and not as an appendage to his wife. The problem was one which not only famous people like Joni had to face. Any couple where one has a disability faces the same issue.

Joni has written in the *English Family* magazine, "The tendency, if you're disabled, is to look on your partner as your nursing attendant. My disability is being used of God to enhance our unity and to illustrate more fully the oneness of our marriage." She valued Ken for his true worth and not as a slightly inferior prince consort, walking a few paces behind on every occasion.

———

Ken and Joni's relationship has grown in a variety of ways since their marriage in 1982. Like any other married couple, they learned that adjustments and compromises had to be made.

"Ken's a keen fisherman and his room holds fishing reels and rods of all sorts. And there are piles of junk everywhere. And it stinks!"

But Joni realizes it's a two-way street.

"My art studio is more cluttered than Ken's fishing room. It has crumpled paint tubes, overflowing wastebaskets . . . smears of water colors on the floor . . . It's my place and I love it!" she admitted.

Joni's disability has facilitated growth in their marriage. In contrast with the inevitable routine of care-giving such as settling Joni in bed for the night, emptying her legbag, brushing her teeth, or cutting up her food, there are special moments that might not otherwise have been shared. Enjoying the intimacy of Ken reading the Bible out loud while she lies in bed is just one example.

"A disability compels open communication. It pushes people to be honest and it presses a husband and wife to resolve their conflicts sooner than most couples do."

Tactless people have been known to say to Ken in front of Joni, "It's amazing that you have given up your life to serve a handicapped woman."

Joni's answer to such comments is loving and yet cuts to the point, leaving no room in the person's mind for disagreement.

"Ken has not given his life to serve a handicapped woman. He's given his life to serve Christ . . . it's just that he's married to someone with a disability."

She teaches the same lesson to people who observe that about her attendants. "They are doing it as to the Lord."

Joni never glosses over the difficulty of living with a disabled person. She realizes how troublesome it can be for families.

"My family survived . . . because God brought along people to help. Sometimes you have to be firm with a handicapped family member if they indulge too much in self-pity, even though they will resent it at first. And you must allow them room for doubt, particularly when the accident or impairment has just happened or just made itself felt. It's only natural—but stand by them to help them when they are ready to start on the road to belief."

"Ken and I have learned to team up against problems . . . we can cope better with them this way. United we stand, but we fall when we're divided."

"Two becoming one flesh isn't a single physical act. It's a long process but well worth the while." Ken and Joni both entered the process with this knowledge and continue to contribute to each other's welfare. Ken's strength and patience are invaluable to Joni. And Joni's supportive and empathetic attitude helps Ken often.

Such an attitude was expressed one night as Joni lay in bed. She heard Ken on the phone in the other room. Though unable to make out the conversation, she could tell by Ken's tone of voice that he was terse and strained. When he finally came into the bedroom and flopped down at the edge of the bed, she was aware that he was worried and preoccupied. "Would it help to tell me about it?" she invited him.

Ken poured out his problem. Joni lay in bed without saying a word for half an hour. She could not offer any advice, but he told her how much better he felt because of her sympathetic ear.

If Ken and Joni ever have something to settle between them, they follow simple rules.

"Fight fair," counsels Joni. "Argue but don't quarrel. Give each other, without interruption, a chance to state their case. Then you can thrash it out from there."

Ken and Joni have never pretended to follow their own rules at all times. Sometimes hurtful remarks are made or unkind actions performed. It is at such times, however, that they seek God's guidance and forgiveness in order to talk through the problem.

Being able to communicate during difficult times has been fostered through sharing in jobs or leisure activities. If Ken was busy in the garden, Joni would wheel out to spend time with him and get involved in the work. Her artistic eye would guide him as he pruned trees and bushes. He would often ask her opinion on plants and color schemes for the flower beds.

Joni also accompanied him to the sports center and cheered him on in his matches. As a competitive sportswoman before her accident, Joni realized how important encouragement and support could be.

Though Joni cannot go out for a long, brisk walk on her own or slip out to the shops to buy a new outfit, she has her own means of recreation. Even though they are not as physically intense as Ken's, the activities do provide a release from pressures.

"It's so much fun to be a painter. One of my favorite times of the day is when I wheel into the art studio. . . . There, a whole new world opens up to me. As an artist, I can express my deepest thoughts and wishes on canvas."

Ken and Joni both love the out-of-doors.

"Getting out into nature is serious business for the Tadas. Yes, my wheelchair limits our excursions, but it doesn't stop us. Ken and I still love to go camping and boating and fishing—or just exploring. It could be the desert . . . or the mountains . . . and then there's the ocean."

Treks with her family and friends figure prominently in her books with vivid descriptions of scenery, wildlife and flora, sunsets, rainbows, waterfalls, and mountains. Each

year they visit Joni's family in Maryland and vacation together in a seaside town called Ocean City.

Viewing all of God's creation and spending time with
Ken has prompted Joni to daydream on occasion.

How lovely it would be to be healed.

Joni had left such wishes in God's hand long ago, but
every once in a while she reflects on what she would like
to be able to do as a wife. Simple chores such as cooking,
cleaning, and washing would be some of the things she
would "enjoy" doing.

Her contentment in Christ's and Ken's love, however,
never allows her to dwell on such daydreams. Though Joni
cannot do many things for Ken, she can still use her mind
and plan things. It is in just such a way that their relationship grows—each one adapting to the situation and learning ways to love the other person.

20

*E*ven a casual observer of Joni's life would admit that God had taken her through a multitude of experiences that fit into His plan of "working all things together for good." The list of trials and opportunities faced by Joni in her life since that dive into Chesapeake Bay is astounding.

More amazing still is to see the changes brought about in her character, attitudes, and in her relationship with God as a result of her experiences. God's means of working all things together for good as described in Romans 8:28 had a purpose—a purpose identified in the verse immediately following: ". . . He predestined to become conformed to the image of His Son . . ." (v. 29).

The contrast in Joni's life now with that of twenty-five years ago exemplifies the grace and wisdom of God. Each change has brought about not only something of benefit and beauty for Joni, it has also brought about something good for disabled people all around the world.

Joni's response to her disability in the first few months had been one of denial and then one of deep bitterness. She had contemplated suicide and even attempted to recruit friends to carry out the task.

By contrast, Joni now sees her disability in the context of God's goodness and her thankfulness. People often remark to Joni, "How can you possibly stand your disability? How can you bear it year in, year out?"

Her reply is always the same.

"It could be worse. My friend Vicky can only shrug her shoulders, whereas I can drive a van. Neither am I in constant pain—that sort of suffering would be far too much for me. But God's grace will be sufficient for your circumstances. He will never test or tempt you beyond what you can bear. Not everyone can be trusted with suffering, but if you have been, accept it and even dare to thank Him for it."

Joni has also grown in her understanding of people's desire to end their life because of their disability. She published a book in 1992 entitled *When Is It Right to Die?* which refuted the arguments posed by so many people in Europe and the U.S. that each person should have a choice as to when to die and that families can make such choices indiscriminately as well as on behalf of their incapacitated loved one.

Joni's book as well as her efforts in opposing legislation in her state of California to permit physician-assisted suicide has thrown Joni into the heat of the battle for the dignity of human life. Such was the wisdom of God in allowing Joni to learn what it was like to want to die.

Joni's attitude toward other disabled people also took a radical turn since her first months after the accident. In those days she had held herself aloof, unwilling to identify with other disabled people. She was particularly offended by the loud, militant ones who were always whining about their rights. She was also uncomfortable with those whose appearance and demeanor were less than lovely.

Gradually, God worked in Joni's life to allow her to see something different.

"I want you to show my love and compassion to these needy people," God's inner voice spoke to Joni.

She wrestled with the idea.

"Don't ask me to do that, Lord. You've got hold of the wrong person."

God's answer was in His Son. She realized that God had sent Jesus to die for those who were unattractive, smelling stale, drooling, and who had twisted bodies, just as much as He had sent Jesus to die for Joni Eareckson.

Joni's change in her view of herself since those early days has also been dramatic. Joni had struggled deeply with her self-image. Through the help of friends and family, Joni realized that God had created her and that her poor self-image was not His plan.

Years later Joni was able to catalog what she was able to do as a result of the confidence that God instilled in her through the encouragement and help of friends.

"I can type, write, and paint with my mouth. I have authored numerous articles and a dozen books, spoken before large audiences, and recorded song albums. I have been the subject of films and videos. I head an international ministry called 'Joni and Friends,' and I host a radio program that is carried on six hundred stations."

Joni's accomplishments were shared in the context of how important other people can be in the life of a disabled person. One's ability to function is dependent upon other people. Simple things in the office and home testify to this truism.

Joni has to borrow hands in order to write a book. "I talk, she types," Joni says about her personal secretary, Francie. Often the ideas flow fast and furious, and even Francie's nimble fingers find it hard to keep up. Sometimes the work slows to a snail's pace because research must be done. In such cases another pair of hands is needed to get the job done.

"I also need someone else to brush my teeth or hold a cup to my lips. . . . Somebody has to tuck in my blouse when it pulls out of my slacks . . . or help me in and out of bed. . . . But it is Jesus who lovingly works through my husband when he helps me in bed at night. And it is Jesus who brings people to help me in the morning."

Jesus also provided people to help her with her self-image. Steve Estes, Diana, Jay, and the therapist, Chris, all contributed to her understanding of her position in Christ or her abilities. One's self-image is very often defined by the kinds of things other people communicate.

God's working in Joni's life to conform her to the image of His Son also affected her relationships with people. Very often during the early years, Joni was self-centered and possessive of people. After painful experiences with her friends Dick and Don, Joni learned the value of letting God be in control.

Years later she would meet and marry a man whom she had given over entirely to God. Praying for the back of his head even before meeting him was indicative of the fact that she had learned that God's will was most important.

Even after her marriage, Joni learned that disappointments were not the end of the story. Ken and Joni, for example, finally realized that though it was possible for a quadriplegic to have a baby, it would not be possible for them. "I got married with the idea of raising children. Again it would have been a question of relying on my friends to help but this dream never materialized. For a while I was heartbroken."

God used the brokenness to channel Ken and Joni's love into ministry with disabled people. And Joni has never lost her love for kids. She has written several children's books, recorded an album for children, and illustrated a children's book. She is surrounded by children wherever she goes.

"Kids are just the right height for hugging," she says.

———————

God's working in Joni's life was not only for her own good. God worked in Joni so that good might come to millions of people. Just as Joni experienced growth, so, too, has her worldwide ministry to people with disabilities.

JAF Ministries, originally known as "Joni and Friends," has grown beyond people's expectations in just twelve years. The ministry was formed to bring the church and disabled people together "through evangelism, encouragement, inspiration, and practical service." While the original purpose is the same, the ministry's activities are varied and span the globe.

Joni's five-minute daily inspirational radio program is heard on over six hundred radio stations. A guidance department answers letters from disabled people and families seeking biblical counsel. The topics of concern range from practical problems such as accessibility to questions regarding God's sovereignty to frustrations regarding the treatment of people with AIDS.

The Christian Fund for the Disabled is an arm of the ministry that provides matching grants to disabled people who need equipment. The fund matches the contribution made by the person's church in order to get the church involved.

Family retreats are conducted in order to provide much-needed rest and encouragement to disabled people and their families. People travel from all over the U.S. for the retreats and go away with new perspectives on their lives.

An important arm of the ministry is called "Field Ministries." Members of the team make it their goal to facilitate the growth of disability ministries across the country. They arrange for meetings at churches, encourage disability ministry workers, and find ways of getting needed resources to such ministries. They also sponsor regional conferences alongside a local sponsor.

Regional conferences are conducted by JAF Ministries. The conferences provide training on a variety of subjects so that Christians can be equipped to meet the needs of people with disabilities.

In addition to serving as the head of the ministry, Joni is directly involved in ministry to disabled people and to people who are assisting disabled people. She does so through numerous speaking engagements, films, books, videos, music, art, and through involvement in organizations such as the Lusanne Conference and the Christian Council on Persons with Disabilities.

JAF Ministries is leading a worldwide effort to reach disabled people. There are 519 million disabled people in the world, most of whom live in third-world countries. If the disabled population were a country, it would rank as the third largest. Disabled people are the least educated, have the least economic resources, have the highest unemployment rate, have the highest divorce rate, and most sadly, are the least evangelized and discipled.

Ministry to this large population was begun many years ago by Joni. She has traveled extensively to over twenty-five countries in the last twelve years. On most occasions, Joni traveled in order to fulfill speaking engagements. While she was there for that purpose, however, it was impossible not to see the many needs faced by disabled people and to meet them face-to-face. And it was impossible not to try to do something.

Worldwide ministry began with simple efforts to provide equipment such as wheelchairs. It also included the translation of her books into foreign languages. But Joni realized that such efforts, while productive in the short term, would not bring about lasting change. Something needed to be done in the hearts of Christians in each country to work among their own disabled people.

A trip to Romania in 1991 was the first step in accomplishing the task. JAF Ministries recruited twenty-five disability ministry professionals from around the U.S. in order to challenge and teach Romanian churches about needs of disabled people. The project had been sparked by reports of cruel and inhumane treatment of disabled children under the former communist regime.

Romania was not the only Eastern European country to undergo change as well as exposure to the way in which disabled people were treated by former leaders. It soon became apparent that conditions in other places were just as alarming.

The news was not all bad, however. At the same time as the new Europe was being formed with the passing of communism, JAF Ministries became increasingly aware of disability ministries starting all over Europe. The strategy became clearer. A catalyst was needed to encourage and train these ministries.

The first step to achieve this objective was to conduct a European Symposium in De Bron, Holland. The conference brought people from all over Europe to attend workshops and plenary sessions.

Joni expressed her aims for the conference. "There are forty-eight million disabled people in the 'new' Europe. That's a lot of folks who need to hear the Gospel of Christ. The Symposium was just one way of fanning the flames of evangelism."

Family magazine reported on the event. "A network of disability ministries has emerged from across the continent, following a meeting of leaders and experts at the

European Symposium on the church and disability. One hundred and eighty delegates from sixteen countries met for training and to share plans and visions for the future."

An office was established in Brussels, Belgium within a year after the Symposium. The team was established in order to continue facilitating disability ministry in Europe through research, networking, and training.

During the time that the European team was being formed, Joni accompanied Billy Graham to Moscow for his crusades. The opportunity was unprecedented both for Dr. Graham and for Joni. It would be the first time in over seventy years that the gospel could be proclaimed so freely to such a large audience. And more importantly, it would pave the way for future outreach to disabled people.

Joni's presence at the crusade brought her in touch with many disabled people. As they had done in Romania, JAF Ministries decided to send a team of people to Russia in order to challenge and teach Christians about disability ministry.

The team went in April of 1993 and saw discouraging conditions. Follow-up trips had to be planned by individual members in order to complete some of the things that had been started during the team's first visit. Relief efforts were organized and training plans put into effect.

Whether speaking on radio or traveling to foreign countries, Joni readily acknowledges that even human hands are not enough to help her. She is dependent upon an even greater hand to help. Prayer is an essential component, not only of Joni's life, but of the entire ministry.

Prayer warriors are an essential part of the ministry and they are all over the globe. The ministry sends out a daily calendar each month with specific prayer requests. Prayer retreats are scheduled to which people who pray regularly for the ministry are invited to come. Prayer warriors even travel with mission teams. Joni has also succeeded in recruiting severely disabled people to pray for other disabled people around the world.

———————

God has not yet completed the good work in Joni Eareckson Tada. There are many days when Joni will admit that she doesn't have it "all together."

"I just want to be with Jesus, get my new glorified body, and have the pain wiped away," Joni confesses readily. And it is not just the physical frustrations that drives Joni to long for heaven. Her battle with temptation and the pain of life contribute to the longing. Most of all, she just wants to see Jesus.

It is this kind of vulnerability that has endeared Joni to so many people. It is also what has made Joni available to God for Him to perform His work in her. In the early days of her paralysis, she wondered if life would have any meaning or if her lifeless hands and feet would ever achieve any good.

A friend quoted a verse from Philippians 1 to her. "He who began a good work in you will carry it on to completion until the day of Christ Jesus."

"Joni, why don't you pray that He will carry out that good work even though you're in a wheelchair?"

She did.

And God has answered her to the glory of His name and to the benefit of millions of people who have gotten to know Joni Eareckson Tada as their friend and as a heroine of the Cross.